Fifth Grade

Everyday Mathematics®

Assessment Handbook

The University of Chicago
School Mathematics Project

Columbus, OH • Chicago, IL • Redmond, WA

The McGraw·Hill Companies

UCSMP Elementary Materials Component

Max Bell, Director

Authors
Jean Bell
William M. Carroll

Acknowledgments
We gratefully acknowledge the work of the following classroom teachers
who provided input and suggestions as we designed this handbook:
Huong Banh, Fran Moore, Jenny Waters, and Lana Winnet.

Photo Credits
Phil Martin/Photography
Cover: Bill Burlingham/Photography
Photo Collage: Herman Adler Design Group

Contributors
Ellen Dairyko, Amy Dillard, Sharon Draznin,
Nancy Hanvey, Laurie Leff, Denise Porter,
Herb Price, Joyce Timmons, Lisa Winters

www.sra4kids.com

 SRA

Send all inquiries to:
SRA/McGraw-Hill
P.O. Box 812960
Chicago, IL 60681

Printed in the United States of America.

ISBN 0-07-600042-7

6 7 8 9 10 POH 08 07 06 05

The **McGraw·Hill** Companies

Contents

Introduction

Too often, school assessment is equated with testing and grading. While some formal assessment is necessary, it tends to provide only scattered snapshots of students rather than records of their growth and progress. The philosophy of *Everyday Mathematics*® is that real assessment should be more like a motion picture, revealing the development of the student's mathematical understanding while giving the teacher useful feedback about instructional needs. Rather than simply providing tests on isolated skills, *Everyday Mathematics* offers a variety of useful techniques and opportunities to assess students' progress on skills, concepts, and thinking processes.

Several assessment tools are built into the *Everyday Mathematics* program. Slate assessments and end-of-unit written assessments are useful in showing how well students are learning the concepts and skills covered in a unit. But these tools by themselves do not provide a balance, highlight progress, or show students' work on larger problems. The purpose of this handbook is to broaden your assessment techniques. Rather than using all of the techniques suggested here, choose a few that balance written work with observation, individual work with group work, and short answers with longer explanations.

For assessment to be valid and useful to both teachers and students, the authors believe that

- teachers need to have a variety of assessment tools and techniques from which to choose.
- students should be included in the assessment process through interviews, written work, and conferences that provide appropriate feedback. Self-assessment and reflection are skills that will develop over time if encouraged.
- assessment and instruction should be closely linked. Assessment should assist teachers in making instructional decisions concerning both individual students and the whole class.
- a good assessment plan makes instruction easier.
- the best assessment plans are those developed by teachers working collaboratively within their schools.

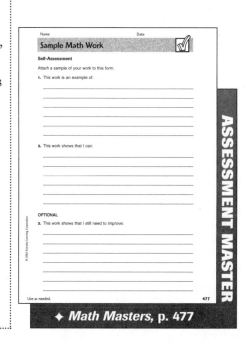

✦ *Math Masters*, p. 477

ASSESSMENT MASTER

This handbook compiles classroom-tested techniques used by experienced *Everyday Mathematics* teachers. It includes suggestions for observing students, keeping anecdotal records, following student progress, and encouraging students to reflect on and communicate both what they have learned and how they feel about mathematics. Many of the assessment suggestions are aimed specifically at *Everyday Mathematics* activities, such as using partner activities and games to observe students and using Math Boxes to focus on a particular concept or skill.

As you read through this handbook, you may want to start with one or two activities that fit your needs and assist you in building a balanced approach to assessment. Feel free to adapt the materials to your own needs. While some teachers find Math Logs useful, others find observations and short, informal interviews more helpful.

The *Everyday Mathematics* goal is to furnish you with some ideas to make assessment and instruction more manageable, productive, and exciting, as well as offer you a more complete picture of each student's progress and instructional needs.

Name   Date

Weekly Math Log

1. What did you study in math this week?

_____

_____

_____

_____

_____

2. Many ideas in math are related to other ideas within math. Think about how the topic(s) you studied in class this week relate to other topics you learned before.

Your reflection can include what you learned in previous years.

_____

_____

_____

_____

_____

_____

_____

_____

474   Use as needed.

ASSESSMENT MASTER

© 2002 Everyday Learning Corporation

◆ *Math Masters, p. 474*

A Balance of Assessments

Ongoing, Product, and Periodic Assessments, and Outside Tests

Although there is no one "right" assessment plan for all classrooms, all assessment plans should use a variety of techniques. To develop your own plan, consider four different assessment sources within the Quad shown in the figure below.

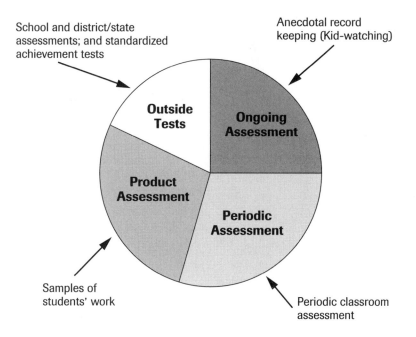

School and district/state assessments; and standardized achievement tests

Anecdotal record keeping (Kid-watching)

Outside Tests

Ongoing Assessment

Product Assessment

Periodic Assessment

Samples of students' work

Periodic classroom assessment

The content of this handbook provides further details about the assessment sources shown in the circle graph. Your own assessment plan should answer these questions:

- *How is the class doing as a whole?*
- *How are individual students doing?*
- *How do I need to adjust instructions to meet students' needs?*
- *How can I communicate to students, parents, and others about the progress being made?*

The proportions of assessment sources shown in the circle graph on page 3 are quite flexible and depend on a number of factors, such as experience of the students and time of year. At the beginning of the year, teachers might use a higher proportion of Ongoing and Product Assessment sources with smaller proportions of Periodic and Outside Test sources.

The section beginning on page 35 provides examples for each unit of how to use different types of assessments in specific lessons.

Ongoing Assessment includes observations of student involvement in regular classroom activities, such as working with partners or small groups during games and working individually on Math Boxes. It may also include observations of students' thinking and shared strategies and information you gather from classroom interactions or from informal individual interviews. Records of these ongoing assessments may take the form of short, written notes; more elaborate record pages; or brief mental notes to yourself. See Ongoing Assessment, pages 13 and 14, for details.

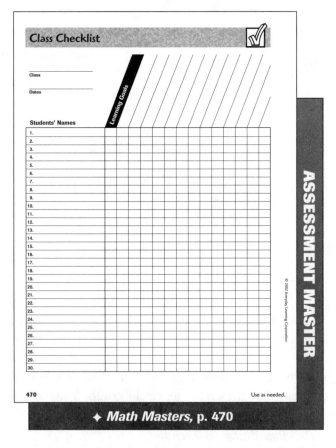

♦ *Math Masters*, p. 470

Product Assessment may include samples of Math Boxes, journal pages, Study Links, solutions to open-ended problems, group project reports, mathematical writing, drawings, sketches, diagrams, and anything else you feel has value and reflects what you want learners to do. If you are keeping portfolios, students should help select which products to include. See Portfolios, page 7, and Product Assessment, pages 15–20.

Periodic Assessment includes more formal assessments, such as end-of-unit assessments, cumulative reviews, quizzes, Class Progress Indicators, and math interest inventories. Pages 21–27 offer suggestions and extensions intended to help you measure both individual and class progress using these types of assessment.

Outside Tests provide information from school, district, state, and standardized tests that might be used to evaluate the progress of a student, class, or school. See page 31 for more information.

A List of Assessment Sources attached to students' folders or portfolios or kept in your record book may help you see whether you have included information from the first three sources of the Quad as well as from other sources. Notice that the completed sample shown below includes only a few of the assessment suggestions from each source. Another teacher might choose other entries. Using multiple techniques will give you a clear picture of each student's progress and instructional needs.

Use this List of Assessment Sources master to keep track of the assessment sources that you are currently using. A blank sample is provided as *Math Masters,* page 468, and is shown in reduced form on page 121 of this book.

> NOTE: Do not try to use all assessment sources at once. Instead, devise a manageable, balanced plan.
>
> Your assessment plan should answer these questions:
> - *How is the class performing as a whole?*
> - *How are individual students performing?*
> - *How can I adjust instruction to meet students' needs?*
> - *How can I communicate to students, parents, and others about the progress being made?*

List of Assessment Sources ☑

Ongoing Assessment
- ✓ Mini mathematical interviews
- ✓ Mental Math and Reflexes
- ✓ Slates

Product Assessment
- ✓ Number-Story Math Log
- ✓ Math Boxes
- ✓ Journals

Periodic Assessment
- ✓ Progress indicators
- ✓ Math Interest Inventories
- ✓ Unit reviews and assessments

Outside Tests
- ✓ State tests

Other

468   Use as needed.

© 2002 Everyday Learning Corporation

Your Assessment Ideas

_____

_____

_____

_____

_____

_____

_____

_____

_____

_____

_____

_____

_____

_____

_____

_____

_____

_____

_____

_____

_____

_____

_____

_____

_____

_____

_____

_____

_____

_____

_____

Your Assessment Ideas

Portfolios

Using Portfolios

Portfolios are used for a number of different purposes, from keeping track of progress to helping students become more reflective about their mathematical growth. The practice of keeping portfolios is a positive assessment technique and is consistent with the philosophy of *Everyday Mathematics* for the following reasons:

- Portfolios emphasize progress over time, rather than results at a given moment. At any time, a student may have Beginning, Developing, or Secure understandings of various mathematical concepts. This progress can best be exhibited by a collection of products organized into portfolios or folders that contain work from different contexts and from different times in the year.

- Portfolios can involve students more directly in the assessment process. Students may write introductions and help select portfolio entries. They can select work they are especially proud of and tag each piece with an explanation of why it was chosen. Developing realistic self-assessment is a valuable skill that takes time to acquire.

- Portfolios can be used as evidence of progress for students, their families, and their teachers for next year. You may want to establish a "Portfolio Night" for students and their parents to attend in order to allow them time to discuss and review portfolio contents. It is very important that parents understand the goals of the various projects and assignments.

- Portfolios can illustrate students' strengths and weaknesses in particular areas of mathematics. Since a rich body of work can be contained in a portfolio, it is a good vehicle for exhibiting each student's progress. Portfolios also can be used to assess students' abilities to see connections within mathematics and to apply mathematical ideas to real-world situations.

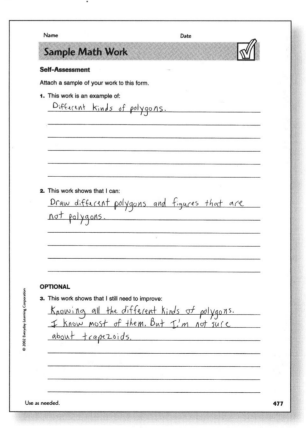

Some teachers keep two types of portfolios: a working portfolio in which students store their recent work and an assessment portfolio. Occasionally, a selection of work is transferred from the working portfolio to the assessment portfolio. Usually, the teacher provides some guidelines for what should be selected, allowing learners to choose within these guidelines.

Many teachers recommend that the number of entries in an assessment portfolio be limited. These entries provide a manageable but representative sample of work. New work can replace old, but some samples from throughout the year should remain.

Listed below are some ideas of representative work that might be included in such a portfolio:

- End-of-unit assessments
- Key assignments
- Student's solutions to challenging problems
- Written accounts of student's feelings about mathematics
- Drawings, sketches, and representations of mathematical ideas and situations
- Photographs of students engaging in mathematics
- Videotapes of students communicating mathematically

For more guidance on developing portfolio assessment, you may wish to consult one of several excellent sources listed on page 33. We especially recommend *Mathematics Assessment: Myths, Models, Good Questions,* and Practical Suggestions, edited by Jean Kerr Stenmark, available through the National Council of Teachers of Mathematics (NCTM). Portfolios, as well as other assessment issues, are also frequently addressed in the NCTM journal *Teaching Children Mathematics.* A video available from NCTM, *Mathematics Assessment: Alternative Approaches,* also discusses portfolios and may be helpful for teachers who are working together to develop a school wide assessment policy.

Name _____ Date _____

Discussion of My Math Work

Self-Assessment

Attach a sample of your work to this page. Tell what you think is important about your sample.

478

Use as needed.

✦ *Math Masters, p. 478*

Ideas in the *Teacher's Lesson Guide*

Portfolio Ideas Samples of students' work may be obtained from the following assignments:

Unit 1

- Exploring a Divisibility Test by 4 (**Lesson 1.5**)
- Investigating Goldbach's Conjecture (**Lesson 1.6**)
- Making Square-Number Collections (**Lesson 1.8**)

Unit 2

- Reading a Book about Estimation (**Lesson 2.1**)
- Finding the Statistical Landmarks for a Set of Data (**Lesson 2.5**)
- Conducting Spinner Experiments (**Lesson 2.6**)
- Exploring an Ancient Multiplication Method (**Lesson 2.9**)
- Solving a Large Number Problem (**Lesson 2.10**)
- Write Place-Value Puzzles (**Lesson 2.11**)

Unit 3

- Reading about Polygons (**Lesson 3.7**)
- Tessellating Quadrangles (**Lesson 3.9**)
- Solving Geometry Template Challenges (**Lesson 3.10**)
- Describe a Polygon (**Lesson 3.11**)

Unit 4

- Writing Division Number Stories (**Lesson 4.5**

Unit 5

- Writing Parts-and-Whole Number Stories (**Lesson 5.1**)
- Finding Fractions of a Whole with Pattern Blocks (**Lesson 5.2**)
- Building Background for Mathematics Words (**Lesson 5.4**)
- Measuring Circle Graphs (**Lesson 5.10**)

Unit 6

- Measuring with a Ruler (**Lesson 6.2**)
- Exploring if the Hand One Writes With Is More Flexible than the Other Hand (**Lesson 6.4**)
- Writing Elapsed Time Number Stories (**Lesson 6.9**)

Unit 7

- Writing Number Stories to Match Expectations (**Lesson 7.4**)

Unit 8

- Writing about Population Trends (**Lesson 8.11**)

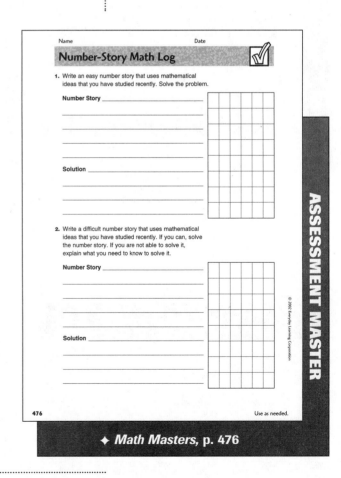

♦ *Math Masters,* p. 476

Unit 9

- Plotting Pictures **(Lesson 9.2)**
- Making Reflected Pictures **(Lesson 9.3)**
- Using the Rectangle Method to Find Areas of Triangles and Parallelograms **(Lesson 9.4)**
- Graphing Survey Results **(Lesson 9.5)**
- Writing Area Number Stories **(Lesson 9.7)**
- Finding the Volume of Prisms **(Lesson 9.9)**
- Plot Pictures **(Lesson 9.11)**
- Write Area Number Stories **(Lesson 9.11)**
- Find the Volume of One Self-Stick Note **(Lesson 9.11)**

Unit 10

- Solving Pan-Balance Problems **(Lesson 10.2)**
- Solving "What's My Rule?" Problems **(Lesson 10.3)**
- Writing Rate Number Stories **(Lesson 10.4)**
- Graphing Values from a Table **(Lesson 10.5)**
- Creating Tables and Graphs **(Lesson 10.5)**
- Write Rate Problems **(Lesson 10.10)**
- Graph Table Values **(Lesson 10.10)**

Unit 11

- Writing Stories about a 2-Dimensional World **(Lesson 11.2)**
- Write Volume Problems **(Lesson 11.8)**
- Exploring Volume by Building Prisms **(Lesson 11.5)**
- Estimating the Volume of a Sheet of Paper **(Lesson 11.5)**
- Modeling the Capacity of Annual Rice Consumption **(Lesson 11.7)**
- Solving a Record Rainfall Problem **(Lesson 11.8)**

Unit 12

- Making Tree Diagrams **(Lesson 12.2)**
- Imagining 10 Times More or 10 Times Less **(Lesson 12.3)**
- Writing Ratio Number Stories **(Lesson 12.5)**
- Write Ratio Number Stories **(Lesson 12.10)**

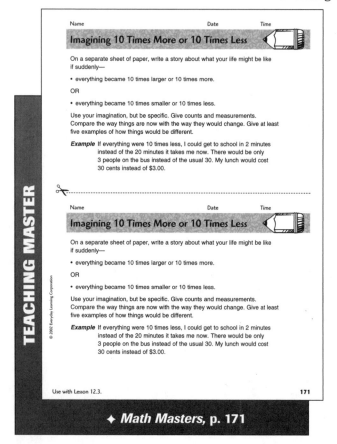

TEACHING MASTER

Name ___ Date ___ Time ___

Imagining 10 Times More or 10 Times Less

On a separate sheet of paper, write a story about what your life might be like if suddenly—

- everything became 10 times larger or 10 times more.

OR

- everything became 10 times smaller or 10 times less.

Use your imagination, but be specific. Give counts and measurements. Compare the way things are now with the way they would change. Give at least five examples of how things would be different.

Example If everything were 10 times less, I could get to school in 2 minutes instead of the 20 minutes it takes me now. There would be only 3 people on the bus instead of the usual 30. My lunch would cost 30 cents instead of $3.00.

Name ___ Date ___ Time ___

Imagining 10 Times More or 10 Times Less

On a separate sheet of paper, write a story about what your life might be like if suddenly—

- everything became 10 times larger or 10 times more.

OR

- everything became 10 times smaller or 10 times less.

Use your imagination, but be specific. Give counts and measurements. Compare the way things are now with the way they would change. Give at least five examples of how things would be different.

Example If everything were 10 times less, I could get to school in 2 minutes instead of the 20 minutes it takes me now. There would be only 3 people on the bus instead of the usual 30. My lunch would cost 30 cents instead of $3.00.

Use with Lesson 12.3. 171

✦ *Math Masters*, p. 171

Rubrics

As most teachers know, learning and understanding are ongoing processes. One good way to keep track of each student's progress is to use a rubric. A rubric is a framework that helps you categorize progress on various aspects of a student's learning. A simple but effective rubric that many teachers use is the classification of students as Beginning, Developing, or Secure with respect to a particular skill or concept. The following rubrics are provided as an introduction to this topic. The most effective rubrics will be those that you and your fellow grade-level teachers tailor to the needs of your students and to the content you are covering.

Sample Rubric
Beginning (B) Students' responses have fragments of appropriate material and show effort to accomplish the task. Students do not explain either the concepts or procedures involved.
Developing (D) Students accomplish part of the task independently. Students can partially explain the process but may need prompting to complete it.
Secure (S) Students' strategies and executions meet the demands of the task and demonstrate a firm grasp of the concepts and procedures involved. Their responses also demonstrate a broad range of understanding, and students apply their understanding in different contexts.

Your own rubric can be modeled after the sample but tailored to meet individual tasks. The sample rubric above can be easily used with any of the sample assessment tools to keep track of the progress of individual students as well as the whole class. You may wish to use the symbols B, D, and S or another set of symbols, such as −, ✓, and +, to chart progress. One teacher suggests using red, yellow, and green color symbols. No matter which rubric symbols you use, a quick look at a completed Class Checklist or a Class Progress Indicator can tell you which areas need further review or which students will benefit from additional help or challenges.

Because some students fall between Developing and Secure or may show exemplary understanding, a 3-point rubric may seem insufficient for some areas you wish to assess. This may be especially true when you are examining performance on a Project or other larger activity. A general five-level rubric follows:

Sample Rubric

Beginning (B)
Students' responses have fragments of appropriate material and show effort to accomplish the task. Students do not explain either the concepts or procedures involved.

Developing (D)
Students accomplish part of the task independently. Students can partially explain the process but may need prompting to complete it.

Developing+ (D+)
Responses convince you that students can revise the work to a Secure performance with the help of feedback (i.e., teacher prompts). While there is a basic understanding, it is not quite Secure or completely independent.

Secure (S)
Students' strategies and executions meet the demands of the task and demonstrate a firm grasp of the concepts and procedures involved. Their responses also demonstrate a broad range of understanding, and students apply their understanding in different contexts.

Secure+ (S+)
A Secure+ performance is exciting. In addition to meeting the qualifications for Secure, a student also merits distinction for special insights, good communication and reasoning, or other exceptional qualities.

Remember, the rubrics are only a framework. When you wish to use a rubric, the general indicators should be made more specific to fit the task, the time of the year, and the grade level at which the rubric is being used. An example of a rubric applied to a specific task is illustrated in this book in the section on Class Progress Indicators beginning on page 22.

Finally, another example of a general rubric follows. This rubric might be applied to a problem in which students are asked both to find an answer and to explain (or illustrate) their reasoning.

Sample Rubric

Level 0
No attempts are made to solve the problem.

Level 1
Partial attempts are made. Reasoning is not explained. Problems are misunderstood or little progress is made.

Level 2
Students arrive at solutions, but solutions are incorrect. However, students clearly show reasoning and correct processes.
or:
Solutions are correct with little or no explanation given.

Level 3
Solutions are correct. Explanations are attempted but are incomplete.

Level 4
Solutions are correct. Explanations are clear and complete.

Level 5
Students give exemplary solutions.

Ongoing Assessment

Observing Students

Observing students during regular classroom interactions, as they work alone and in groups, is an important assessment technique in *Everyday Mathematics*. The methods described can help you manage ongoing observations. A discussion of record-keeping follows.

Teacher-Guided Instruction

During the lesson, circulate around the room, interacting with the students and observing the mathematical behavior that is taking place. Identify those students who are having difficulty or showing progress. Be alert to significant comments and interactions. These quick observations often tell a great deal about a student's mathematical thinking. Practice making mental notes on the spot, and follow them up with brief written notes when possible. The important thing is to find an efficient way to keep track of students' progress without getting overwhelmed with papers, lists, and notes.

Mathematical Mini-Interviews

Observing and listening to students as they work will enable you to note progress. However, there are times when brief verbal interactions with probing questions clarify and enhance observations. These brief, nonthreatening, one-on-one interactions, overheard by the rest of the class or conducted in private, encourage mathematical communication skills. They should apply to the content at hand during any instructional interaction.

Games

At the beginning of the year, when children are first becoming comfortable with *Everyday Mathematics* games, and while they are working in small groups, circulate around the classroom observing the strategies that students are employing. Once students are playing the games independently, use the time to work with a small group having difficulty. Use recording tools to note any valuable information regarding individual mathematical development. You can also use this time to conduct mathematical mini-interviews.

Mental Math and Reflexes

As you present the class with Mental Math and Reflexes situations, focus on a small group of students, perhaps five at a time. You should never feel that all students need to be observed every day.

Strategy Sharing

Over time, encourage each student to share his or her strategies while working at the board or overhead projector. It is during this time that you should assume the role of "guide on the side" rather than "sage on the stage." In the *Everyday Mathematics* classroom, many strategies are used; recording students' strategies will help you know how to address individual strengths and needs.

Slates

Periodically, record students' responses from their slate reviews. The *Teacher's Lesson Guide* offers suggested problems. You may begin with these problems or make up your own. Slate assessment offers both review and a quick assessment of students' progress toward computation mastery. You might focus on one group at a time and indicate only those students with Beginning understanding. Provide follow-up instruction for them based on your records.

Recording Observations

When observing students, you may use a number of recording tools to organize your observations. The following suggestions may be helpful to you. Choose one that appeals to you most and try it. If necessary, adapt it to make it more useful or try another tool.

Computer Labels

Print out students' names on sheets of large computer address labels. Write observations on the appropriate labels. As labels become filled, place them on numbered file cards and file them sequentially throughout the year.

Seating Charts or Calendar Grids

Place each student's name in a grid cell and write observations in the cells as you circulate throughout the classroom. After reflecting on whole-class needs, cut apart the cells, date them, and file them for each student. Or use self-stick notes in the cells. Replace full notes with new ones to avoid having to cut out cells. Use the notes to analyze individual strengths and needs and to prepare for parent conferences.

Class Checklists

A blank Class Checklist is provided in *Math Masters,* page 470. A mini version is shown on page 122 of this book. You may want to use it for recording ongoing observations and interactions by identifying a particular learning goal and using a rubric symbol to indicate students' progress on the checklist.

Product Assessment

Products from *Everyday Mathematics*

Samples of students' mathematical writings, drawings, and creations add balance to the assessment process. This section offers a review of some of the products that are part of *Everyday Mathematics,* as well as suggestions for outside sources for product assessment. Some of these items can be selected and stored in a portfolio or work folder along with other assessments.

Math Journals

Math Journals can be considered working portfolios. Students should keep the journals intact so that they can revisit, review, correct, and improve their responses at a later time. You and students might select journal pages focusing on topics of concern or story problems or those featuring open-ended tasks to photocopy and include in portfolios. Some journal pages can be used to record information about long-term projects and reports on American Tour activities. You may access these pages to document students' progress on number collections, equivalent names for fractions, and scores on 50-facts tests. Two other types of journal pages that can be used as assessment are Math Boxes and Time to Reflect.

Math Boxes

Math Boxes are an important routine for reviewing and maintaining skills. They also offer an excellent opportunity for ongoing assessment, providing glimpses into how a student performs in several areas. References in the *Teacher's Lesson Guide* identify paired Math Boxes pages and tell which problems cover prerequisites for the next unit.

One method for record keeping when assessing work with Math Boxes is to circulate and make informal observations on a copy of the Math Boxes page. Record names and comments about individuals who are having difficulties on self-stick notes placed over individual Math Boxes.

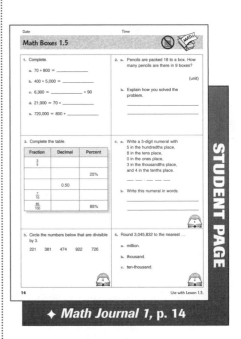

♦ *Math Journal 1,* p. 14

Time to Reflect

These self-assessment journal pages offer students an opportunity to reflect on their progress. These single-page activities include two or three open-ended questions that lead students to decide which concepts they are finding easy, difficult, or surprising. Students might be asked how they would teach a concept or skill. Some questions simply ask students to critique their own performance. Student responses on these pages can provide a useful insight into students' mathematical reasoning skills.

Additional Assessment Products

Many teachers are interested in gathering examples of students' writing and thinking in addition to those provided by *Everyday Mathematics* materials. This type of writing is usually more open-ended and allows teachers more flexibility in topics while they provide students with opportunities to reflect on, assess their understanding, and enhance their communication skills. This section provides examples of products you may wish to include in your assessment plan.

Math Logs

Some teachers find it beneficial for students to write about mathematics regularly. A spiral notebook or a set of log sheets can be used as a math log. (See sample masters in *Math Masters,* pages 472–474.) Not only can these written reflections serve as a powerful means of checking students' understanding, but they are also a means of assessing curiosity, persistence, risk taking, and self-confidence.

Remember that math logs are not "end products" but, instead, are an important part of the ongoing assessment process referred to in the Introduction. They are helpful to both you and students only if they reveal useful feedback and encourage the development of mathematical thinking, understanding, and written communication.

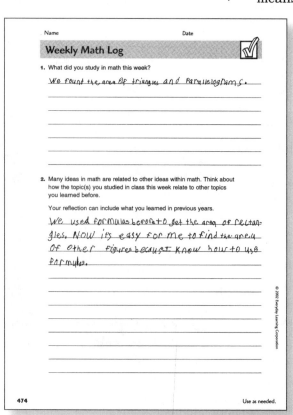

Here are some suggestions on how to encourage students to write:

Open-Ended Questions Use open-ended questions to start students writing. Some prompts that you can use are

- *What does the term (range, landmark, square root) mean?*
- *What is (division, π)? Give an example of when you use it.*
- *Why is this answer right (wrong)? Explain.*
- *How do you know your answer is correct?*
- *What was your strategy for finding the solution?*
- *How many ways can you find a solution for this problem?*
- *Find the error in the following problem. Why is it an error?*
- *How is this like something you have learned before?*

Students may use Exit Slip sheets to record responses to open-ended questions at the close of a lesson or unit. (See *Math Masters*, page 479.)

Number Stories Occasionally ask students to write a number story. Sometimes you may wish to supply the numbers. For example:

- *Write a number story that uses the numbers $\frac{2}{3}$ and 0.5.*
- *Write a number story that uses all square numbers less than 10.*

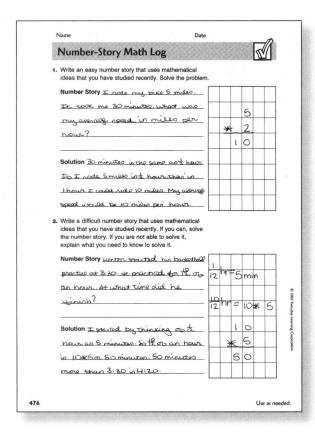

At other times, you may leave the instructions more open-ended:

- *Make up a number story using square units.*
- *Write a number story that uses a variable.*

Written number stories provide concrete assessment of students' understanding of operations, relationships, and numbers. For example, students might choose the incorrect operation to find an answer. Number stories often point out misconceptions.

Portfolio Writing If you are using portfolios, students can write entries for their portfolios. To help focus the writing, you might suggest that they write about one of the following topics:

- *What I Hope to Learn about Mathematics This Year*
- *Why Mathematics Is Important*
- *My Plan for Learning Mathematics*

As the year continues and entries change, ask students to update their introductions and tell why they have chosen the different pieces. At the end of the year, students could re-evaluate their portfolios and make a list of important concepts that they have learned.

Concept and Strategy Writing Prior to the teaching of a unit, invite students to share what they already know about the concepts being presented. For example, before you teach a unit on division, students could reflect in response to these questions or topics:

- *What is division?*
- *When do you use division?*
- *Write an example of the toughest kind of division problem you can solve. Then solve the problem.*
- *Write an example of a division number story.*

The answers to these questions/statements may help you plan your instruction. At the close of each unit, ask students to respond to the same statements or questions. This technique allows students and you to compare growth in understanding of the concepts. You may even discover a need to clear up some students' misconceptions.

Students can use words, representations, or both to explain their thinking. Communicating about mathematics encourages students to reflect upon their thinking and provides you with another window into their thought processes. Model this kind of writing on the overhead to show students how to use this format.

Alternatives to Math Logs

Even if you do not want to have students keep regular math logs, have them occasionally write about mathematics so they can develop their writing skills. During each unit, give students short writing assignments. Writing topics can be based on any of the math log suggestions given, or they can be short reflections written just before the end-of-unit assessment. For example:

- *The math I know best / least in this unit is _____.*
- *Uses for the mathematics I learned in this unit are _____.*

These assignments could also be more content-oriented. For example:

- *About how many miles is it from your home to your school?*
- *About how many footsteps would you have to take to get from your home to your school?*
- *Describe what you did to estimate the number of footsteps you would take.*

Try to include students in the assessment process. The products listed below will encourage students to develop their ability to think reflectively. These products can be used as Math Messages or Math Boxes within the program or in math logs or alternatives to math logs.

Reflective Writing and Self-Assessment

Open-ended statements and questions, such as those suggested here, provide students with opportunities to reflect on what they know and what they do not know. Invite students to reflect before, during, and/or after a lesson. Here are some prompts you can use:

- *My goal for tomorrow is ...*
- *I learned that ...*
- *I was surprised that I ...*
- *I was pleased that I ...*
- *I still don't understand ...*
- *Because of the mathematics lesson today, I feel more confident about ...*
- *The most important thing I learned in Everyday Mathematics today (this week) is ...*
- *I think (percents, calculators) are ...*
- *(Multiplication) is easy if ...*
- *The trouble with mathematics is ...*
- *What I like most (or least) about Lesson X is ...*
- *How would you explain to an absent student what we did today?*
- *What was the most difficult (easiest) part of today's lesson?*
- *Write a test problem that I might give to see if you understand today's lesson.*
- *What did you learn today that you did not know before?*
- *What did you like or dislike about today's lesson? Why?*

NOTE: Do not feel discouraged if students have difficulty communicating mathematically. This is a skill that takes time to develop.

Students who begin the year having nothing to say or who answer in short, incomplete sentences become much more fluent as the year progresses.

How often should you use a math log or other writing in your math program? This depends on you and your students. While some teachers use logs a few times per week, you may find that once a week (perhaps on Friday, reflecting on what students did that week) or at the end of the unit is sufficient.

Choose the amount of additional writing with which you and your students feel comfortable.

Sometimes you may want students to focus on how they worked in a small group:

- *What worked well in your group today?*
- *Describe what your job was in your group today.*
- *What could you have done to help your group work better?*
- *What do you like or dislike about working in a group?*

End-of-Year Reflection This kind of writing may give teachers some ideas about students' attitudes toward mathematics and about which experiences have been the most beneficial. Responses will vary, depending on the writing ability and reflective experiences of the students.

I enjoyed math in 5th grade. What I like best is working with data. Last year I learned how to figure the range, median, and mode of a set of data. This year I learned how to draw circle graphs and measure pieces of circle graphs. When you look at a circle graph, it's easy to understand the data.

I often look in my journals when I want to see all the things I learned this year. My journals help me to review also.

There are so many things that we studied in 3rd and 4th grade that I used this year. I think I'll like math next year too. That's why I know that what I learned in math this year will help me next year.

Periodic Assessment

Periodic assessment activities are those that are done at fairly consistent times or intervals over the school year. We will briefly review periodic assessment sources that are currently part of *Everyday Mathematics* and then discuss additional sources that experienced teachers use.

Sources from Everyday Mathematics

Unit Reviews and Assessments

Each unit of your *Teacher's Lesson Guide* ends with a review and assessment lesson that lists the learning goals for that unit. The goals list is followed by a cumulative review that includes suggestions for oral and slate assessments as well as group or independent written assessment ideas and performance assessment activities. Assessment lessons also include a self-assessment page called "Time to Reflect" in students' journals.

This cumulative oral, slate, and written review provides an opportunity for you to check students' progress on concepts and skills that were introduced or further developed in the unit. In addition to these resources, other suggestions include

- Use rubrics to record progress toward each learning goal you assess. Rubrics are introduced on pages 11 and 12 of this book, and examples of how to use them are provided on pages 22–24 and in the unit Assessment Overviews section beginning on page 35.

- Only a few of the concepts and skills from any unit are suggested for assessment at the end of each unit. You should feel free to add items that you believe need assessing. You may also wish to delete items with which students are Secure.

- Since many of the end-of-unit reviews and assessments tend to focus on skills, you may want to add more concept-oriented and open-ended questions as suggested in the Product Assessment section of this book, beginning on page 15.

- You could accumulate information from the skills lists (in the review and assessment lessons) and then add them to the Quarterly Class Checklists and Individual Profiles of Progress.

Assessing Students' Journal Work

You might use rubrics to periodically assess pages within journals as independent reviews. Also, several activities throughout the journals have students glue their best work onto the page. You might develop a rubric to assess these activities as well.

By recording your individual objectives on a Class Progress Indicator or a Class Checklist, you can ascertain which students may need additional experience. These students can then be paired with students who are proficient in that particular skill or activity.

Midyear and End-of-Year Assessments

The Midyear and End-of-Year Assessment Masters (*Math Masters,* pages 414–426) provide additional assessment opportunities that you may wish to use as part of your balanced assessment plan. Minis of these masters, with answers, are shown on pages 94–100 of this book. These tests cover important concepts and skills presented in Fifth Grade *Everyday Mathematics,* but they are not designed to be used as "pretests," and they should not be your primary assessment tools. Use them along with the ongoing, product, and periodic assessments that are found within the lessons and at the end of each unit.

Additional Sources for Periodic Assessment

Class Progress Indicators

Class Progress Indicators, also known as Performance Charts, are another assessment tool that some teachers have found useful in assessing and tracking students' progress on selected mathematical topics.

A Class Progress Indicator form provides space to record students' performance on any mathematical topic you choose to assess two or three times during the year.

The first assessment opportunity, which usually occurs after students have some exposure to and experience with a topic, provides a baseline for your students' performance early in the year. By recording the second and third assessments on the same form, you can track the progress of each student as well as the whole class throughout the school year. A fifth grade teacher's sample Class Progress Indicator is shown on page 23. A blank form of this master is provided in *Math Masters,* page 471.

Class Progress Indicator

Mathematical Topic Being Assessed: _Determine Value of a Variable_

	BEGINNING	DEVELOPING OR DEVELOPING+	SECURE OR SECURE+
First Assessment After Lesson: _4.6_ Dates included: _11/1_ to _11/4_	Molly Eric Gloria John	Tim James Ellie Natalia Norman Claire Allison Josepha	Ben Christi
Second Assessment After Lesson: _5.8_ Dates included: _12/9_ to _12/13_	Eric Gloria	John James Ellie Natalia Norman Claire Allison Tim	Josepha Ben Christi
Third Assessment After Lesson: _____ Dates included: _____ to _____			

Notes

_____

_____

_____

_____

© 2002 Everyday Learning Corporation

Use as needed.   **471**

Record the names of students under the columns that best indicate their ability levels: Beginning, Developing, or Secure, or whatever rubric symbols you like to use. If you wish, use (+) to indicate students who are between these levels. As you conduct your assessments, keep this question in mind: What do I need to do instructionally to promote progress? Space is provided at the bottom of the form for any notes you may wish to make.

Below is an example of a mathematical topic and an accompanying rubric.

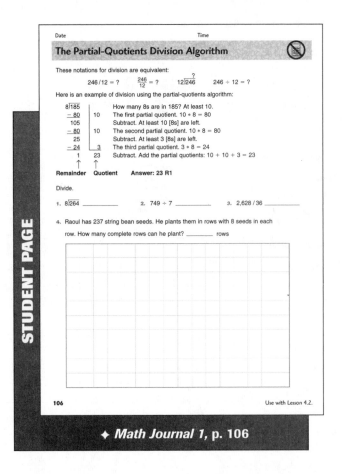

Date   Time

The Partial-Quotients Division Algorithm

These notations for division are equivalent:

$$246/12 = ? \qquad \frac{246}{12} = ? \qquad 12\overline{)246}^{\,?} \qquad 246 \div 12 = ?$$

Here is an example of division using the partial-quotients algorithm:

$8\overline{)185}$		How many 8s are in 185? At least 10.
$-\,80$	10	The first partial quotient. $10 * 8 = 80$
105		Subtract. At least 10 [8s] are left.
$-\,80$	10	The second partial quotient. $10 * 8 = 80$
25		Subtract. At least 3 [8s] are left.
$-\,24$	3	The third partial quotient. $3 * 8 = 24$
1	23	Subtract. Add the partial quotients: $10 + 10 + 3 = 23$

Remainder   Quotient   **Answer: 23 R1**

Divide.

1. $8\overline{)264}$ _____   2. $749 \div 7$ _____   3. $2,628/36$ _____

4. Raoul has 237 string bean seeds. He plants them in rows with 8 seeds in each
   row. How many complete rows can he plant? _____ rows

106   Use with Lesson 4.2.

♦ *Math Journal 1*, p. 106

Sample Division Algorithm Rubric

Beginning (B)
Students find some correct solutions but do not explain their algorithms or account for remainders. Students may use a different algorithm for each problem since they have not yet found one algorithm they prefer.

Developing (D)
Students find correct solutions and account for remainders. They use one procedure more often than any other and are able to explain the algorithm they use most often.

Secure (S)
Students find correct solutions, including accounting for all remainders. Students have chosen a preferred algorithm and can explain their algorithm to others.

Remember, the more experience you have with the range of students' responses, the easier it will be to determine or assign rubrics.

Class Checklists and Individual Profiles of Progress

To help you keep track of students' progress in areas that are important to your school and district, the authors of *Everyday Mathematics* have provided learning goals checklists for individuals and for the class. These Class Checklists and Individual Profiles of Progress are provided for each unit as well as for each quarter. They are found at the back of your *Math Masters* book on pages 428–467 and are reproduced in a reduced version in the Assessment Masters section of this book on pages 101–121.

The checklists identify learning outcomes for each unit of *Everyday Mathematics* and indicate the approximate level of proficiency expected: *Beginning, Developing,* or *Secure.* For many of the learning goals, the level is identified as "Developing" rather than "Secure." "Developing" topics have been included so that you can record student progress over time.

Many of these learning goals are assessed at the end of each unit; all of them are developed on journal pages. You may want to use the checklists to help you give priorities to lesson materials.

The checklists assume that students had *Everyday Mathematics* in earlier grades. You may need to make adjustments for students who used other mathematics programs.

First, use the Class Checklists to gather and record information. Then, transfer selected information to the Individual Profiles of Progress sheet for each student's portfolio or for use during parent conferences.

The information recorded on the checklists can be obtained from end-of-unit oral and written assessments. In fact, you may want to bypass the Class Checklists and record this information from these assessments directly onto the Individual Profiles of Progress.

✦ *Math Masters*, p. 448

✦ *Math Masters*, p. 449

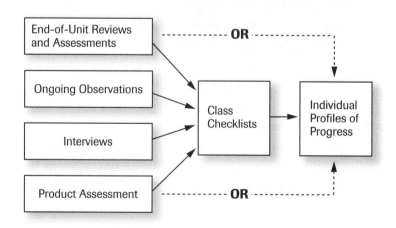

Blank profile and checklist masters can be found in *Math Masters,* pages 469 and 470. You may wish to record information from other sources, such as journal review pages, Math Boxes, Math Messages, and math logs.

Information obtained from teacher-directed instruction is also a good resource to be recorded on the Class Checklists or directly on Individual Profiles of Progress. As mentioned in the Ongoing Assessment section of this book, information can also be obtained from observations, questions, and other sources during regular instructional interactions.

Individual Mathematical Interviews

Periodic interviews of ten to fifteen minutes with each student are a splendid idea and will prove valuable and revealing. They are, however, very difficult to carry out, given the full classroom schedule and the need to provide supervision for the rest of the class.

A compromise would be at least one goal-oriented, five-minute talk with each student during the year. At the start of the year, the interview might focus on the student's preparation for the content to come. At midyear, the interview might be concerned with how the work in mathematics has been going. Near the year's end, it might involve the student's preparation for next year.

The interview can be conducted while the rest of the class is playing mathematical games or working independently. Teachers have also suggested that, if it is feasible, you can make "appointments" to have lunch with students individually or with two or three students at a time. Other appointments might be arranged before class begins, during recess, or after school.

The following are suggested questions for a midyear interview:

• *How do you feel about mathematics?*

• *What have you enjoyed most about mathematics?*

• *What has been the easiest (hardest) part of mathematics for you?*

• *How can we work together to help you feel more comfortable with these difficult parts of mathematics?*

• *How do you feel about working with partners and in small groups for some mathematics activities?*

You might also consider interviewing students about their responses to Time to Reflect questions. Students' responses might be recorded on paper or tape-recorded.

"My Math Class" Inventories

At the beginning of the year, you may want students to complete an inventory to assess their mathematical attitudes. This inventory might be repeated later in the year to see whether their attitudes have changed. Two samples (Evaluating My Math Class; My Math Class) are shown below. Blank masters of these inventories are found in *Math Masters*, pages 472 and 473. Inventories can be included in students' portfolios and discussed during individual interviews or parent conferences.

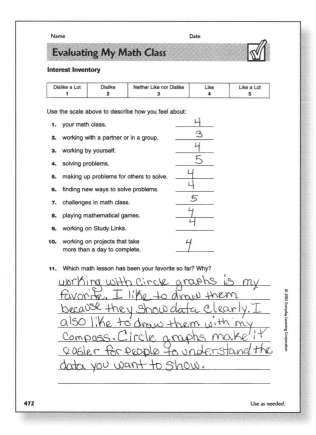

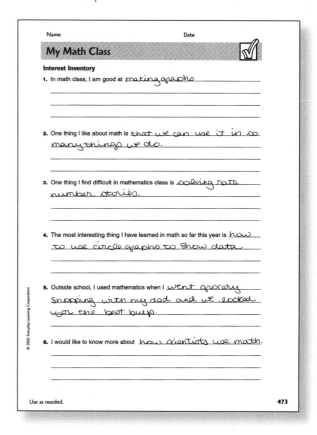

Your Assessment Ideas

Grading

Traditionally, the main purpose of end-of-unit assessments is to help the teacher monitor student progress and evaluate student achievement. In addition, end-of-unit assessments in *Everyday Mathematics* provide valuable information for planning future lessons.

The philosophy behind the end-of-unit assessments agrees with that expressed in the NCTM *Assessment Standards for School Mathematics* (1995). The diagram below, which is taken from that publication, illustrates how the four purposes of assessment translate into classroom practices:

Four Purposes of Assessment and Their Results

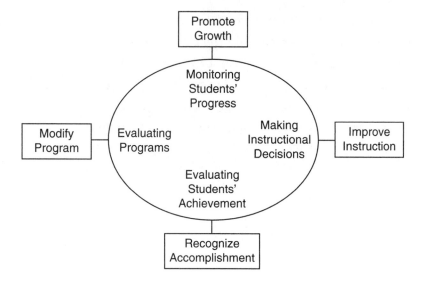

Because *Everyday Mathematics* presents concepts and skills repeatedly throughout the year, it is important to know how students are progressing individually on a concept or skill, as well as how much the class as a whole understands it. For that reason, the end-of-unit assessments in *Everyday Mathematics* include items at an exposure step of the spiral, in addition to items that assess mastery.

On the basis of students' performance on these assessment tools, teachers can make informed decisions about how to approach concepts and skills in future lessons. For example, several students may correctly answer a question on fraction addition, but the class as a whole is not Secure at it. The teacher knows that the next time the skill appears in the spiral, he or she can call on student leaders to help get the class started.

Since end-of-unit assessments have several purposes, they should not be the only source for grades. Following are some of the ways to accumulate scores for student grades:

- Create open-ended problems or use those that are in the journal. Grade the answers to these problems according to a rubric that assigns points to the different performance levels.
- Record scores on cumulative reviews.
- Record scores on review masters.
- Develop interim quizzes.
- Assign points for successful group problem solving.
- Weigh the value of questions on the end-of-unit assessments, checking progress according to your expectations for mastery.

This list is only a beginning. Assessment is as individual as are teaching styles. While developing your own assessment plan for *Everyday Mathematics,* consider the following guidelines:

- Start small.
- Define unit objectives to be assessed.
- Incorporate assessment into the class routine.
- Set up an easy and efficient record-keeping system.
- Personalize and adapt the plan as the year progresses.

Everyday Mathematics provides regular opportunities to assess student progress. Choose those that best match your teaching style and students' needs.

Outside Tests

Outside tests are generally tests given at the school, district, or state level, or they are nationally standardized tests. Most teachers are familiar with the standardized tests that have multiple-choice responses. The frustrating aspect of this type of test is that it analyzes a narrow range of mathematical thinking and doesn't assess the depth and breadth of the mathematical knowledge that should be attained in a well-implemented *Everyday Mathematics* classroom.

There are ways to help your students function well in testing environments. Math Boxes, for example, can be tailored to help prepare students for the formats of an outside test. Even without such preparation, *Everyday Mathematics* students generally do about as well on the computation sections of standardized tests and much better on concepts and problem-solving sections, as students in traditional programs.

More recently, performance assessments or open-ended tests have been developed. These tests report results similar to those from traditional tests—class and individual norms (percentile rankings)—but they also attempt to test problem solving and communication skills on larger tasks. Some of these tests provide rubric scores along with normed data. Try to encourage the use of one of these newer performance-based tests at the district level rather than the traditional multiple-choice tests.

Performance-based assessments developed at the school or district level probably afford the best opportunity to reflect the instructional practices in local classrooms. Teams of teachers and administrators can develop assessments and rubrics that enhance the learning process rather than focus on narrow thinking used only in a small portion of mathematical activities. At some grade levels, these assessments can be used exclusively. When standardized testing is mandatory at a certain grade level, these assessments can give a better picture of the mathematical education occurring in the classroom.

Your Assessment Ideas

_____

_____

_____

_____

_____

_____

_____

_____

_____

_____

_____

_____

_____

_____

_____

_____

_____

_____

_____

_____

_____

_____

_____

_____

_____

Recommended Reading

Black, Paul, and Dylan Wiliam. "Assessment and Classroom Learning." *Assessment in Education* (March, 1998): 7–74.

———. "Inside the Black Box: Raising Standards Through Classroom Assessment." *Phi Delta Kappan* 80, no. 2 (October, 1998): 139–149.

Bryant, Brian R., and Teddy Maddox. "Using Alternative Assessment Techniques to Plan and Evaluate Mathematics." *LD Forum* 21, no. 2 (winter, 1996): 24–33.

Eisner, Elliot W. "The Uses and Limits of Performance Assessment." *Phi Delta Kappan* 80, no. 9 (May, 1999): 658–661.

Kuhn, Gerald. *Mathematics Assessment: What Works in the Classroom.* San Francisco: Jossey-Bass Publishers, 1994.

National Council of Teachers of Mathematics (NCTM). *Curriculum and Evaluation Standards for School Mathematics.* Reston, Va.: NCTM, 1989.

———. *Assessment Standards for School Mathematics.* Reston, Va.: NCTM, 1995.

———. *Principles and Standards for School Mathematics.* Reston, Va.: NCTM, 2000.

National Research Council, Mathematical Sciences Education Board. *Measuring What Counts: A Conceptual Guide for Mathematics Assessment.* Washington, D.C.: National Academy Press, 1993.

Pearson, Bethyl, and Cathy Berghoff. "London Bridge Is Not Falling Down: It's Supporting Alternative Assessment." *TESOL Journal* 5, no. 4 (summer, 1996): 28–31.

Shepard, Lorrie A. "Using Assessment to Improve Learning." *Educational Leadership* 52, no. 5 (February, 1995): 38–43.

Stenmark, Jean Kerr, ed. *Mathematics Assessment: Myths, Models, Good Questions, and Practical Suggestions.* Reston, Va.: National Council of Teachers of Mathematics, 1991.

Stiggens, Richard J. *Student-Centered Classroom Assessment.* Englewood Cliffs, N.J.: Prentice-Hall, 1997.

Webb, N. L., and A. F. Coxford, eds. *Assessment in the Mathematics Classroom: 1993 Yearbook.* Reston, Va.: National Council of Teachers of Mathematics, 1993.

Your Assessment Ideas

_____

_____

_____

_____

_____

_____

_____

_____

_____

_____

_____

_____

_____

_____

_____

_____

_____

_____

_____

_____

_____

_____

_____

_____

_____

_____

_____

Assessment Overviews

This section offers examples of how to use different types of assessments in specific lessons. For each unit, you will find examples of three major types of assessment opportunities: Ongoing Assessment, Product Assessment, and Periodic Assessment. Keep in mind, however, that these are not distinct categories; they frequently overlap. For example, some Periodic Assessments may also serve as Product Assessments that you or the student may choose to keep in the student's portfolio.

Unit 1
Assessment Overview

There are many pathways to a balanced assessment plan. As you teach Unit 1, start to become familiar with some of the approaches to assessment. The next few pages provide examples of the three major types of assessment suggested in this program: Ongoing Assessment, Product Assessment, and Periodic Assessment. This assessment overview offers examples of ways to assess students on what they learn in Unit 1. Do not try to use all of the examples, but begin with a few that meet your needs.

Ongoing Assessment Opportunities

Ongoing assessment provides opportunities to observe students during regular interactions as they work independently and in groups. You can conduct ongoing assessment during teacher-guided instruction, Math Boxes sessions, mathematical mini-interviews, games, Mental Math and Reflexes sessions, strategy sharing, and slate work. The chart below provides a summary of ongoing assessment opportunities in Unit 1 as they relate to specific Unit 1 learning goals.

1c	**Developing/Secure Goal** Use a divisibility test to determine if a number is divisible by another number. (Lesson 1.5)	Lesson 1.1, p. 16 Lesson 1.5, p. 34
1d	**Developing/Secure Goal** Identify prime and composite numbers. (Lessons 1.6 and 1.9)	Lesson 1.1, p. 16
1e	**Developing/Secure Goal** Understand how square numbers and their square roots are related. (Lesson 1.8)	Lesson 1.1, p. 16 Lesson 1.8, p. 48
1f	**Secure Goal** Draw arrays to model multiplication. (Lessons 1.2 and 1.7)	Lesson 1.3, p. 25
1g	**Secure Goal** Know multiplication facts. (Lessons 1.2–1.9)	Lesson 1.1, p. 16 Lesson 1.4, p. 29

Product Assessment Opportunities

Math Journals, Math Boxes, Activity Sheets, *Math Masters,* math logs, and the results of Projects all provide product assessment opportunities. Here is an example of how you might use a rubric to assess a student's ability to make square-number collections.

Lesson 1.8, p. 49

EXTRA PRACTICE **Making Square-Number Collections**

Students collect representations of a square number. Students write representations of equivalent values, using arrays, multiplication expressions, and expressions containing exponents or square root symbols. The sample rubric below can help you evaluate students' work.

Portfolio Ideas

Sample Rubric
Beginning (B) Independently, the student creates a collection for a specified square number. However, the student is relying on basic operations such as $50 + 50 = 100$ or $1{,}000/100 = 10$. He or she does not apply the concepts of exponents and square roots. The student generates less than 10 equivalencies.
Developing (D) Independently, the student creates a collection for a specified square number. He or she moves beyond utilizing basic operations by applying concepts emphasized in the unit. The student draws arrays, utilizes exponents, and writes multiplication expressions and square roots. The student generates a collection of 10 or more equivalencies.
Secure (S) Independently, the student creates a collection for a specified square number. He or she generates equivalencies that apply concepts within the unit and beyond. For example, the student will begin to use expressions with exponents such as $20^2 - 10^2 - 10^2 - 10^2$, or $5^2 * 2^2$. The student generates a collection beyond 10 equivalencies.

Periodic Assessment Opportunities

Here is a summary of the periodic assessment opportunities that are provided in Unit 1. Refer to Lesson 1.10 for details.

Oral and Slate Assessment

In Lesson 1.10, you will find slate assessment problems on pages 57 and 58.

Written Assessment

In Lesson 1.10, you will find written assessment problems on pages 58 and 59 (*Math Masters,* pages 379 and 380).

See the following chart to find slate and written assessment problems that address specific learning goals.

1a	**Beginning Goal** Find the prime factorizations of numbers. (Lesson 1.9)	Written Assessment, Problems 6 and 7
1b	**Beginning/Developing Goal** Rename numbers written in exponential notation. (Lessons 1.7–1.9)	Written Assessment, Problems 7 and 8
1c	**Developing/Secure Goal** Use a divisibility test to determine if a number is divisible by another number. (Lesson 1.5)	Slate Assessment, Problem 4 Written Assessment, Problems 11, 12, and 14
1d	**Developing/Secure Goal** Identify prime and composite numbers. (Lessons 1.6 and 1.9)	Slate Assessment, Problem 3 Written Assessment, Problems 4, 5, 13, and 14
1e	**Developing/Secure Goal** Understand how square numbers and their square roots are related. (Lesson 1.8)	Slate Assessment, Problem 1 Written Assessment, Problem 8
1f	**Secure Goal** Draw arrays to model multiplication. (Lessons 1.2 and 1.7)	Written Assessment, Problem 1
1g	**Secure Goal** Know multiplication facts. (Lessons 1.2–1.9)	Written Assessment, Problems 1, 4, and 8
1h	**Secure Goal** Identify even and odd numbers. (Lessons 1.4 and 1.5)	Slate Assessment, Problem 3 Written Assessment, Problems 2 and 13
1i	**Secure Goal** Find the factors of numbers. (Lessons 1.3, 1.4, 1.6, and 1.9)	Written Assessment, Problems 3, 9, and 10

Alternative Assessment

In Lesson 1.10, you will find alternative assessment options on page 60.

✦ Play *Beat the Calculator*

Assess students' reflex multiplication skills by having them play the game *Beat the Calculator.* Collect records of student success with this game in order to identify the facts for which each student needs more practice.

✦ Play *Factor Captor*

To assess a student's ability to identify factors of a number as well as to distinguish between prime and composite numbers, play the *Factor Captor* game. On an Exit Slip, have each student describe what he or she thinks is a winning strategy for the game.

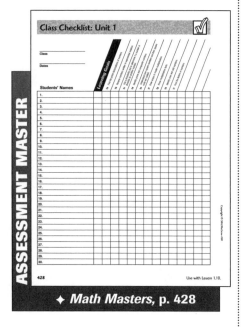

✦ Math Masters, p. 428

Unit 2
Assessment Overview

If you tried some of the assessment approaches that were suggested in the Unit 1 Assessment Overview, you are probably beginning to appreciate how the goal charts in this section can help you plan your assessment strategies. For example, at this point students are expected to be at a Secure level for finding the sum and difference of multidigit whole numbers and decimals (see Goal 2f in the chart below). The chart alerts you to the fact that an ongoing assessment opportunity related to that goal is provided in Lesson 2.3 on page 90 of your *Teacher's Lesson Guide*. In similar fashion, you can use the chart on page 41 to find written assessment opportunities related to this same goal.

Ongoing Assessment Opportunities

Ongoing assessment provides opportunities to observe students during regular interactions as they work independently and in groups. You can conduct ongoing assessment during teacher-guided instruction, Math Boxes sessions, mathematical mini-interviews, games, Mental Math and Reflexes sessions, strategy sharing, and slate work. The chart below provides a summary of ongoing assessment opportunities in Unit 2 as they relate to specific Unit 2 learning goals.

2d **Developing/Secure Goal** Find the product of multidigit whole numbers and decimals. (Lessons 2.8 and 2.9)	Lesson 2.8, p. 117 Lesson 2.9, p. 123
2e **Developing/Secure Goal** Know place value to billions. (Lesson 2.10)	Lesson 2.10, p. 128
2f **Secure Goal** Find the sum and difference of multidigit whole numbers and decimals. (Lessons 2.2 and 2.3)	Lesson 2.3, p. 90
2g **Secure Goal** Identify the maximum, minimum, median, mode, and mean for a data set. (Lesson 2.5)	Lesson 2.5, p. 101

Product Assessment Opportunities

Math Journals, Math Boxes, Activity Sheets, *Math Masters,* math logs, and the results of Projects all provide product assessment opportunities. Here is an example of how you might use a rubric to assess a student's ability to write place-value puzzles.

Lesson 2.11, p. 132

ALTERNATIVE ASSESSMENT **Write Place-Value Puzzles**

Mastery of place-value concepts is essential to an understanding of large numbers. This activity gives students an opportunity to apply their understanding of place value by writing place-value puzzles. The puzzle in *Math Masters,* page 13, provides a model for students. Use your own rubric or the sample rubric below to evaluate students' work.

> ### Sample Rubric
>
> **Beginning (B)**
> The student attempts to create a place-value puzzle but needs assistance in getting started. Once the student begins, he or she uses a simple whole number requiring basic clues. The student generates simple clues or ones that are incorrect. For example: 9 - 5; write the answer in the ones place.
>
> **Developing (D)**
> The student creates a place-value puzzle independently. He or she selects a target number that may involve decimals or is a larger whole number. The written clues are more complex and possibly involve more than one operation or other mathematical concepts. For example: Multiply the digit in the thousands place by the digit in the millions place; subtract 5 from the result; write the answer in the tens place. Some information may be missing, making it difficult to complete the puzzle.
>
> **Secure (S)**
> The student creates a place-value puzzle independently. The written clues incorporate a wide range of mathematical concepts. Students may give clues that involve fractions, measurements of angles, exponents, divisibility, and so forth. The target number involves decimals and/or large numbers such as millions. It is evident that the student is proficient in his or her understanding of a variety of mathematical concepts, including place value.

Periodic Assessment Opportunities

Here is a summary of the periodic assessment opportunities that are provided in Unit 2. Refer to Lesson 2.11 for details.

Oral and Slate Assessment

In Lesson 2.11, you will find slate assessment problems on page 131.

Written Assessment

In Lesson 2.11, you will find written assessment problems on page 132 (*Math Masters,* pages 381–383).

See the following chart to find slate and written assessment problems that address specific learning goals.

2a **Beginning Goal** Write and solve open sentences for number stories. (Lesson 2.4)	Written Assessment, Problem 19
2b **Developing Goal** Round numbers to designated places. (Lesson 2.7)	Slate Assessment, Problem 1 Written Assessment, Problems 7–10
2c **Developing/Secure Goal** Make magnitude estimates. (Lesson 2.7)	Written Assessment, Problems 14–17
2d **Developing/Secure Goal** Find the product of multidigit whole numbers. (Lessons 2.8 and 2.9)	Slate Assessment, Problem 2 Written Assessment, Problems 12–17
2e **Developing/Secure Goal** Know place value to billions. (Lesson 2.10)	Slate Assessment, Problem 3 Written Assessment, Problem 11
2f **Secure Goal** Find the sum and difference of multidigit whole numbers and decimals. (Lessons 2.2 and 2.3)	Written Assessment, Problems 1–6
2g **Secure Goal** Identify the maximum, minimum, median, mode, and mean for a data set. (Lesson 2.5)	Written Assessment, Problem 18

Alternative Assessment

In Lesson 2.11, you will find alternative assessment options on pages 132 and 133.

✦ **Write Place-Value Puzzles**

Use the suggestions and rubric on page 40 to assess students' understanding of place value by having them write place-value puzzles.

✦ **Play *Subtraction Target Practice***

As students play this game from Lesson 2.3, you will have an opportunity to assess their subtraction skills. Collect students' records from at least one round of the game, then use a Class Checklist to tally their ability levels. Alternatively, you can circulate and use Calendar Grids to record their subtraction skills.

✦ **Play *Number Top-It***

As students play this game, have them record their five numbers for each round in order from least to greatest. Collect these records after five rounds to assess their ability to order large numbers. Keep questions like the following in mind:

• Does the student order the numbers properly from least to greatest?

• If not, is there any pattern to the order in which the numbers are placed?

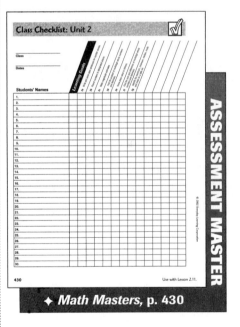

✦ *Math Masters, p. 430*

Unit 3
Assessment Overview

At this stage in their learning, most of your fifth-grade students should be either at a Secure level or still Developing many of the geometry learning goals in this unit. A major focus of this unit is on angles. The chart below indicates that there are two ongoing assessment opportunities related to one of these goals, 3c, which is measuring angles. They can be found in Lesson 3.4 on pages 162 and 163 of your *Teacher's Lesson Guide.* Similarly, the chart on page 43 indicates where you can find written problems to gauge students' progress toward this same goal.

Ongoing Assessment Opportunities

Ongoing assessment provides opportunities to observe students during regular interactions as they work independently and in groups. You can conduct ongoing assessment during teacher-guided instruction, Math Boxes sessions, mathematical mini-interviews, games, Mental Math and Reflexes sessions, strategy sharing, and slate work. The chart below provides a summary of ongoing assessment opportunities in Unit 3 as they relate to specific Unit 3 learning goals.

3a **Developing Goal** Determine angle measures based on relationships between angles. (Lessons 3.3–3.5 and 3.9)	Lesson 3.3, p. 156 Lesson 3.9, p. 189
3c **Developing/Secure Goal** Measure an angle to within 2°. (Lessons 3.4 and 3.9)	Lesson 3.4, pp. 162 and 163
3d **Developing/Secure Goal** Identify types of angles. (Lessons 3.4 and 3.5)	Lesson 3.5, p. 168

Product Assessment Opportunities

Math Journals, Math Boxes, Activity Sheets, *Math Masters,* math logs, and the results of Projects all provide product assessment opportunities. On the next page is an example of how you might use a rubric to assess a student's familiarity with the attributes of polygons.

ALTERNATIVE ASSESSMENT Describe a Polygon

A good way to assess students' knowledge of the attributes of polygons is to have them draw polygons and figures that are not polygons. Use your own rubric, or the following sample rubric, to evaluate students' work.

Portfolio Ideas

Sample Rubric
Beginning (B)   The student has difficulty generating attributes of polygons without teacher assistance or referral to the *Student Reference Book*. The student may write "has 4 sides," listing an attribute of a quadrangle versus that of a polygon. As a result, the student only draws polygons with 4 sides under "polygon," and other polygons under "not polygons." In other words, the student is still in the process of comprehending the attributes of polygons.
Developing (D)   The student generates a list of one or two attributes of polygons. He or she is able to generate more attributes with assistance from the *Student Reference Book*. He or she draws at least two figures for each category of "polygons" and "not polygons."
Secure (S)   The student demonstrates proficiency with the attributes of polygons by listing four or more attributes without referring to the *Student Reference Book*. He or she draws at least three or more examples of "polygons" and "not polygons."

Periodic Assessment Opportunities

Here is a summary of the periodic assessment opportunities that are provided in Unit 3. Refer to Lesson 3.11 for details.

Slate Assessments

In Lesson 3.11, you will find slate assessment problems on pages 198 and 199.

Written Assessment

In Lesson 3.11, you will find written assessment problems on pages 199 and 200 (*Math Masters,* pages 384–386).

See the following chart to find slate and written assessment problems that address specific learning goals.

3a **Developing Goal** Determine angle measures based on relationships between angles. (Lessons 3.3–3.5 and 3.9)	Written Assessment, Problems 1–3
3b **Developing/Secure Goal** Estimate the measure of an angle. (Lessons 3.6 and 3.8)	Slate Assessment, Problem 5 Written Assessment, Problems 8, 17, and 18
3c **Developing/Secure Goal** Measure an angle to within 2°. (Lessons 3.4 and 3.9)	Written Assessment, Problems 4–6

3d	**Developing/Secure Goal** Identify types of angles. (Lessons 3.4 and 3.5)	Slate Assessment, Problem 5 Written Assessment, Problems 4–8, 17, and 18
3e	**Developing/Secure Goal** Identify types of triangles. (Lesson 3.6)	Written Assessment, Problems 10–14
3f	**Secure Goal** Identify place value in numbers to billions. (Lesson 3.2)	Slate Assessment, Problem 3 Written Assessment, Problem 9
3g	**Secure Goal** Know properties of polygons. (Lesson 3.7)	Written Assessment, Problems 13–14, 17, and 18
3h	**Secure Goal** Define and create tessellations. (Lesson 3.8)	Written Assessment, Problems 15 and 16

Alternative Assessment

In Lesson 3.11, you will find alternative assessment options on page 200.

✦ **Play** *Angle Tangle*

This game can help you assess a student's ability to estimate and measure angles. The game is played in pairs. One player draws an angle and the other player estimates the size of the angle. The first player then measures the angle. As you observe students playing the game, use the following questions to help you assess students' progress.

• Can each student measure angles accurately?

• Are their estimates and actual measurements far apart?

✦ **Play** *Polygon Capture*

In this game, students draw attribute cards and match polygon cards to the attribute. As you observe students playing the game, use a Class Checklist or Calendar Grids to record students' progress. Keep the following questions in mind:

• Does the student quickly recognize a polygon with the given attribute?

• Does the student recognize all polygons that fit?

• Can the student rule out polygons that do not have the attribute?

✦ **Describe a Polygon**

Use the rubric on page 43 to assess students' knowledge of polygon attributes.

Portfolio Ideas

✦ *Math Masters, p. 432*

ASSESSMENT MASTER

Unit 4
Assessment Overview

At this point in the *Everyday Mathematics* program, you may wish to consider whether you are beginning to establish a balance of Ongoing, Product, and Periodic Assessment strategies. Also, think about whether your strategies include both anecdotal records based on observations of students' progress and the use of written assessments.

Ongoing Assessment Opportunities

Ongoing assessment provides opportunities to observe students during regular interactions as they work independently and in groups. You can conduct ongoing assessment during teacher-guided instruction, Math Boxes sessions, mathematical mini-interviews, games, Mental Math and Reflexes sessions, strategy sharing, and slate work. The chart segment below provides a summary of ongoing assessment opportunities in Unit 4 as they relate to specific Unit 4 learning goals.

Developing Goal Interpret the remainder in division number stories. (Lesson 4.5)	Lesson 4.5, p. 239

Product Assessment Opportunities

Math Journals, Math Boxes, Activity Sheets, *Math Masters,* math logs, and the results of Projects all provide product assessment opportunities. On the next page is an example of how you might use a rubric to assess a student's ability to write division number stories.

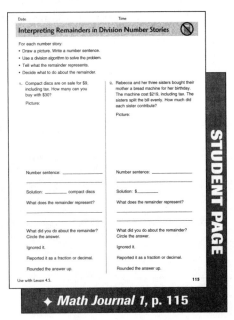

♦ *Math Journal 1,* p. 115

Lesson 4.5, p. 240
ENRICHMENT Writing Division Number Stories

A good way to assess students' understanding of division is to have students write division number stories. Use your own rubric, or the sample rubric below, to evaluate students' work.

Sample Rubric

Beginning (B)
The student attempts to write a division number story but experiences difficulty due to a lack of understanding of the concept of division. Teacher assistance is required. The student may write a simple division problem involving a basic fact or fact extension such as 30/5 = 6, or 300/60 = 5.

Developing (D)
Without teacher assistance, the student writes a division number story that displays an understanding of division. He or she uses a 1- or 2-digit divisor and at least a 3-digit dividend. The number story does not include a remainder to be considered when solving the problem.

Secure (S)
The student writes a division number story that displays a Secure understanding of division. He or she uses a 1- or 2-digit divisor and at least a 3-digit dividend. The number story requires the remainder to be considered when solving the problem.

Periodic Assessment Opportunities

Here is a summary of the periodic assessment opportunities that are provided in Unit 4. Refer to Lesson 4.7 for details.

Slate Assessment

In Lesson 4.7, you will find slate assessment problems on pages 246 and 247.

Written Assessment

In Lesson 4.7, you will find written assessment problems on page 247 (*Math Masters*, pages 387 and 388).

See the following chart to find slate and written assessment problems that address specific learning goals.

4a **Beginning Goal** Divide decimal numbers by whole numbers with no remainders. (Lessons 4.4 and 4.5)	Written Assessment, Problems 7 and 8
4b **Beginning/Developing Goal** Write and solve number sentences with variables for division number stories. (Lessons 4.5 and 4.6)	Written Assessment, Problems 9, 10, and 13
4c **Developing Goal** Find the quotient and remainder of a whole number divided by a 1-digit whole number. (Lessons 4.1, 4.2, 4.4, and 4.5)	Written Assessment, Problems 1–4, 9, 10, and 13
4d **Developing Goal** Find the quotient and remainder of a whole number divided by a 2-digit whole number. (Lessons 4.2, 4.4, and 4.5)	Written Assessment, Problems 5 and 6

4e	**Developing Goal** Make magnitude estimates for quotients of whole and decimal numbers divided by whole numbers. (Lessons 4.4 and 4.5)	Written Assessment, Problems 7 and 8
4f	**Developing Goal** Interpret the remainder in division number stories. (Lesson 4.5)	Written Assessment, Problems 9 and 10
4g	**Developing Goal** Determine the value of a variable; use this value to complete a number sentence. (Lesson 4.6)	Written Assessment, Problems 11 and 12
4h	**Secure Goal** Know place value to hundredths. (Lesson 4.1)	Slate Assessment, Problems 1 and 3

Alternative Assessment

In Lesson 4.7, you will find alternative assessment options on page 248.

✦ Practice with Fact Families

Students complete Fact Triangles for multiplication and division. As students complete *Math Masters,* page 38, use a Class Checklist or Calendar Grids to record students' progress. Keep the following questions in mind:

• Does the student understand the relationship between multiplication and division?

• Is the student confident with multiplication facts? With division facts?

✦ Play *Division Dash*

Use this game to assess students' knowledge of dividing a 2-digit number by a 1-digit number. Students use the square root key on a calculator to generate random numbers—a 1-digit divisor and a 2-digit dividend. Students do not use the calculator to divide. Students play alone or with a partner. They play until one of the players has quotients that have a sum of 100. As students play the game, keep the following questions in mind:

• Can the student estimate the quotient?

• Was the student able to use mental math to find any of the quotients?

• Is the student proficient with the division algorithm?

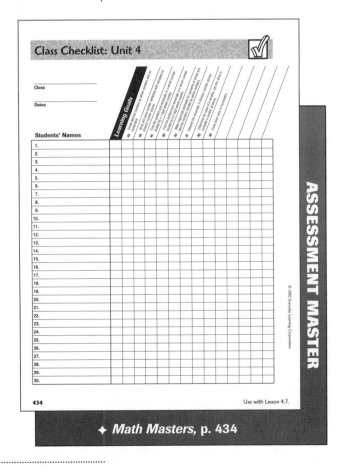

✦ *Math Masters,* p. 434

✦ Play *First to 100*

Use this game to assess a student's ability to solve open-number sentences. Students use cards in *Math Masters,* pages 46 and 47. As students play the game, keep the following questions in mind:

• Does the student understand the variable *x?*

• Is he or she able to solve a simple number sentence for *x?*

• Can the student write a simple number sentence to help solve a word problem?

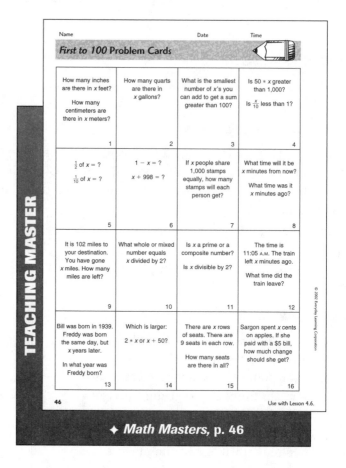

✦ *Math Masters,* p. 46

Unit 5
Assessment Overview

In this unit, students further develop their ability to work with fractions. Depending on the specific skill, students' ability levels might range from Beginning to Secure. A good mix of ongoing assessment opportunities is suggested in the chart below for several learning goals that deal with fractions. Written and slate assessments for these same goals are listed in the chart on pages 50 and 51.

Ongoing Assessment Opportunities

Ongoing assessment provides opportunities to observe students during regular interactions as they work independently and in groups. You can conduct ongoing assessment during teacher-guided instruction, Math Boxes sessions, mathematical mini-interviews, games, Mental Math and Reflexes sessions, strategy sharing, and slate work. The chart below provides a summary of ongoing assessment opportunities in Unit 5 as they relate to specific Unit 5 learning goals.

5c **Developing Goal** Convert between fractions and percents. (Lesson 5.8)	Lesson 5.8, p. 309
5d **Developing Goal** Draw a circle graph for a set of data. (Lesson 5.11)	Lesson 5.11, p. 324
5e **Developing Goal** Measure pieces of a circle graph; interpret a circle graph. (Lesson 5.10)	Lesson 5.10, p. 319
5g **Developing/Secure Goal** Find equivalent fractions. (Lesson 5.4)	Lesson 5.4, p. 284

Product Assessment Opportunities

Math Journals, Math Boxes, Activity Sheets, *Math Masters,* math logs, and the results of Projects all provide product assessment opportunities. Here is an example of how you might use a rubric to assess a student's ability to describe what fraction of the whole the part is.

Lesson 5.2, p. 273

RETEACHING ### Finding Fractions of a Whole with Pattern Blocks

Most of your students should be able to visualize what fractional part of a whole shape a fraction block would cover, but ability levels will vary. Some students may need to use the pattern-block shapes or make sketches to find the answer. Use your own rubric, or the sample rubric below, to evaluate students' work.

Portfolio Ideas

Sample Rubric
Beginning (B)
The student experiences difficulty getting started, and teacher assistance is required. He or she requires the use of pattern blocks to arrive at a correct solution. The student may experience some difficulty in making the transfer to Shape B. As a result, some of the pattern-block pieces will be labeled with incorrect fractions.
Developing (D)
The student completes the activity independently. He or she completes Shape A by visualizing the appropriate pattern blocks needed and the value for each. The questions for Shape B require the student to use some of the pattern blocks or create a sketch to cover the shape in order to record the value of each block.
Secure (S)
The student completes the activity independently. He or she completes both sets of questions by visualizing the value of each pattern-block shape. The student has no difficulty transferring from one representation for a "whole" to another.

Periodic Assessment Opportunities

Here is a summary of the periodic assessment opportunities that are provided in Unit 5. Refer to Lesson 5.13 for details.

Slate Assessment

In Lesson 5.13, you will find slate assessment problems on pages 333 and 334.

Written Assessment

In Lesson 5.13, you will find written assessment problems on pages 334 and 335 (*Math Masters*, pages 389–391).

See the following chart to find slate and written assessment problems that address specific learning goals.

5a	**Beginning/Developing Goal** Add fractions with like denominators. (Lesson 5.3)	Written Assessment, Problems 12–14
5b	**Developing Goal** Order and compare fractions. (Lesson 5.3)	Written Assessment, Problems 15–20
5c	**Developing Goal** Convert between fractions and percents. (Lesson 5.8)	Slate Assessment, Problem 2 Written Assessment, Problem 8

5d	**Developing Goal** Draw a circle graph for a set of data. (Lesson 5.11)	Written Assessment, Problem 23
5e	**Developing Goal** Measure pieces of a circle graph; interpret a circle graph. (Lesson 5.10)	Written Assessment, Problems 21, 22, and 24–26
5f	**Developing/Secure Goal** Convert between fractions and mixed numbers. (Lesson 5.2)	Slate Assessment, Problems 4 and 5 Written Assessment, Problems 4–7 and 9–11
5g	**Developing/Secure Goal** Find equivalent fractions. (Lesson 5.4)	Slate Assessment, Problem 6 Written Assessment, Problems 1–3

Alternative Assessment

In Lesson 5.13, you will find alternative assessment options on pages 335 and 336.

✦ Play *2-4-5-10 Frac-Tac-Toe*

Use *Math Masters,* pages 62, 63, and 66 to assess a student's ability to convert between fractions and decimals or between fractions and percents, depending on which version you use. As students work with partners to play the games, keep the following questions in mind:

• Can the student recognize a fraction equal to 0 or 1?

• Is the student able to use a calculator to find the appropriate decimal or percent?

• Is the student able to recognize that a decimal or a percent is greater than a given decimal or percent?

✦ Identify Fractions in Pattern-Block Designs

Students work with partners to make pattern-block designs. Then they trade with their partners and find the value of their partner's designs. This activity helps you assess their facility with finding fractional parts of a whole and their ability to convert between improper fractions and mixed numbers. As students work, keep these questions in mind:

• Can the student fit the pattern-block shapes exactly over his or her partner's design?

• Did the student correctly identify the fraction for each shape in the design?

• Is the student able to add the fractions to find the value of the design?

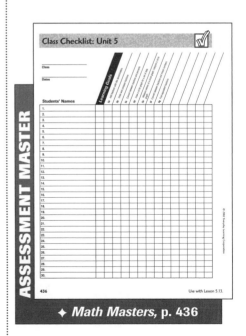

✦ *Math Masters,* p. 436

Unit 6
Assessment Overview

The focus of this unit is organizing data. The goal chart below shows ongoing assessment opportunities for observing students as they develop this skill. For example, to see how well students are progressing with Goal 6b, the chart shows that ongoing assessment opportunities related to this goal can be found in Lessons 6.3, 6.4, and 6.10 on pages 365, 370, and 401 of your *Teacher's Lesson Guide*. The chart on page 54 indicates where you can find slate and written problems to help you assess students' progress toward this same goal.

Ongoing Assessment Opportunities

Ongoing assessment provides opportunities to observe students during regular interactions as they work independently and in groups. You can conduct ongoing assessment during teacher-guided instruction, Math Boxes sessions, mathematical mini-interviews, games, Mental Math and Reflexes sessions, strategy sharing, and slate work. The chart below provides a summary of ongoing assessment opportunities in Unit 6 as they relate to specific Unit 6 learning goals.

6b **Beginning/Developing Goal** Read and interpret stem-and-leaf plots. (Lesson 6.4)	Lesson 6.3, p. 365 Lesson 6.4, p. 370 Lesson 6.10, p. 401
6c **Developing Goal** Add and subtract fractions with like denominators. (Lessons 6.8–6.10)	Lesson 6.8, p. 391
6d **Developing Goal** Add and subtract fractions with unlike denominators. (Lessons 6.8–6.10)	Lesson 6.9, p. 396
6f **Developing Goal** Find common denominators. (Lessons 6.9 and 6.10)	Lesson 6.9, p. 396
6h **Secure Goal** Identify and use data landmarks. (Lessons 6.1, 6.5, and 6.6)	Lesson 6.10, p. 401

Product Assessment Opportunities

Math Journals, Math Boxes, Activity Sheets, *Math Masters,* math logs, and the results of Projects all provide product assessment opportunities. Here is an example of how you might use a rubric to assess a student's ability to measure angles.

Lesson 6.4, p. 370

Exploring If the Hand One Writes With Is More Flexible Than the Other Hand

Most of your students should be able to trace their left and right hands and measure the angles formed by the index fingers and thumbs. Some students may have trouble following the instructions to draw and measure the correct angles. Use your own rubric, or the sample rubric below, to evaluate students' work.

Sample Rubric
Beginning (B)
The student begins the activity independently by tracing his or her right and left hand. He or she may require teacher assistance in order to make the appropriate angle formed by the thumb and little finger. As a result, the angles drawn may be incorrect. The student also experiences difficulty in measuring the angles formed by using a protractor. As a result, the measurements are incorrect.
Developing (D)
The student traces his or her right and left hand independently. He or she attempts to draw the angles formed by the thumb and little finger. Some assistance may be required. The student attempts to measure the angles formed but requires some guidance when using the protractor. As a result, one of the measurements may be incorrect.
Secure (S)
The student traces his or her right and left hand independently. The angles that are formed by the thumb and little finger are drawn correctly. The student uses his or her protractor to measure angles with accurate measurements.

Periodic Assessment Opportunities

Here is a summary of the periodic assessment opportunities that are provided in Unit 6. Refer to Lesson 6.11 for details.

Slate Assessment

In Lesson 6.11, you will find slate assessment problems on pages 404 and 405.

Written Assessment

In Lesson 6.11, you will find written assessment problems on pages 405 and 406 (*Math Masters,* pages 392–394).

See the following chart to find slate and written assessment problems that address specific learning goals.

6a	**Beginning/Developing Goal** Construct stem-and-leaf plots. (Lesson 6.3)	Written Assessment, Problem 22
6b	**Beginning/Developing Goal** Read and interpret stem-and-leaf plots. (Lesson 6.4)	Written Assessment, Problems 7 and 22
6c	**Developing Goal** Add and subtract fractions with like denominators. (Lessons 6.8–6.10)	Written Assessment, Problems 9, 11, and 17c
6d	**Developing Goal** Add and subtract fractions with unlike denominators. (Lessons 6.8–6.10)	Written Assessment, Problems 10, 12–16, and 17b
6e	**Developing Goal** Understand how sample size affects results. (Lesson 6.5)	Written Assessment, Problems 5b, 5c, and 8e
6f	**Developing Goal** Find common denominators. (Lessons 6.9 and 6.10)	Written Assessment, Problems 12–16, 17b, and 18–20
6g	**Developing/Secure Goal** Convert between fractions, decimals, and percents. (Lessons 6.5, 6.8, and 6.10)	Slate Assessment, Problems 2, 4, and 5 Written Assessment, Problems 6 and 8b–8d
6h	**Secure Goal** Identify and use data landmarks. (Lessons 6.1, 6.5, and 6.6)	Written Assessment, Problems 1–5, 7, and 21

Alternative Assessment

In Lesson 6.11, you will find alternative assessment options on page 406.

✦ Create a Set of Data for Given Data Landmarks

This activity is intended to assess students' understanding of data landmarks. Students create their own data sets given a maximum, minimum, median, and mode. Consider the following questions:

- Does the student begin the activity by arranging the 4 numbers he or she is given?
- Does the student understand the meaning of *maximum, minimum, median,* and *mode*?
- Does the data set have the correct maximum, minimum, median, and mode?

✦ Add and Subtract Fractions with Pattern-Block Models

This activity in *Math Masters,* page 86, helps you assess students' facility with finding fractional parts of a whole, with adding and subtracting fractions, and their abilities to convert between improper fractions and mixed numbers. Use a Class Checklist or Calendar Grid to record students' progress. As students work, keep these questions in mind:

- Did the student correctly identify the fraction for each shape?
- Was the student able to design a shape with a given value?
- Could the student write a number sentence to describe how to find the value for his or her design?

Class Checklist: Unit 6

Class

Dates

Students' Names

438   Use with Lesson 6.11.

✦ Math Masters, p. 438

Unit 7
Assessment Overview

In this unit, students begin their study of exponential notation and further develop their abilities to work with positive and negative numbers. Depending on the specific skill, students' ability levels might range from Beginning to Secure. A good mix of ongoing assessment opportunities is suggested in the chart below for several learning goals that deal with fractions. Written and slate assessments for these same goals are listed in the chart on page 57.

Ongoing Assessment Opportunities

Ongoing assessment provides opportunities to observe students during regular interactions as they work independently and in groups. You can conduct ongoing assessment during teacher-guided instruction, Math Boxes sessions, mathematical mini-interviews, games, Mental Math and Reflexes sessions, strategy sharing, and slate work. The chart below provides a summary of ongoing assessment opportunities in Unit 7 as they relate to specific Unit 7 learning goals.

7a	**Beginning/Developing Goal** Understand and apply scientific notation. (Lesson 7.3)	Lesson 7.3, p. 516
7b	**Developing Goal** Understand and apply powers of 10. (Lesson 7.2)	Lesson 7.2, p. 510
7c	**Developing Goal** Understand and apply order of operations to evaluate expressions and solve number sentences. (Lesson 7.5)	Lesson 7.5, p. 527
7d	**Developing Goal** Add and subtract integers. (Lessons 7.7–7.10)	Lesson 7.7, p. 540 Lesson 7.8, p. 545
7e	**Developing/Secure Goal** Understand and apply exponential notation. (Lessons 7.1 and 7.2)	Lesson 7.1, p. 504
7g	**Developing/Secure Goal** Understand the function and placement of parentheses in number sentences. (Lesson 7.4)	Lesson 7.4, p. 522
7h	**Developing/Secure Goal** Compare and order integers. (Lesson 7.6)	Lesson 7.6, pp. 533 and 534

Product Assessment Opportunities

Math Journals, Math Boxes, Activity Sheets, *Math Masters,* math logs, and the results of Projects all provide product assessment opportunities. Here is an example of how you might use a rubric to assess a student's ability to write number stories.

Lesson 7.4, p. 523

EXTRA PRACTICE **Write Number Stories to Match Expressions**

Most of your students should be able to write number stories for the given expression, but ability levels will vary. Some students can write creative, complicated stories, others just simple ones. Use your own rubric, or the sample rubric below, to evaluate students' work.

Sample Rubric
Beginning (B)
The student requires teacher assistance to write a number story that matches a given expression. The story does not match one of the two versions of expressions given or the story does not go with the expression for which it is intended. For example, the student writes a number story for $(7 * 5) - 4 = 31$, but it actually matches $7 * (5 - 4) = 7$ or another similar expression.
Developing (D)
The student attempts to independently write a number story for one of the two versions of expressions given. He or she writes a simple number story that matches the intended expression.
Secure (S)
The student writes number stories independently. He or she writes number stories that match each of the given expressions. The student will also write more complex stories.

Periodic Assessment Opportunities

Here is a summary of the periodic assessment opportunities that are provided in Unit 7. Refer to Lesson 7.11 for details.

Slate Assessment

In Lesson 7.11, you will find slate assessment problems on pages 560 and 561.

Written Assessment

In Lesson 7.11, you will find written assessment problems on pages 561 and 562 (*Math Masters,* pages 395–397).

See the following chart to find slate and written assessment problems that address specific learning goals.

7a **Beginning/Developing Goal** Understand and apply scientific notation. (Lesson 7.3)	Slate Assessment, Problem 3 Written Assessment, Problems 1–4
7b **Developing Goal** Understand and apply powers of 10. (Lesson 7.2)	Slate Assessment, Problem 2 Written Assessment, Problems 1–4
7c **Developing Goal** Understand and apply order of operations to evaluate expressions and solve number sentences. (Lesson 7.5)	Written Assessment, Problems 19–28
7d **Developing Goal** Add and subtract integers. (Lessons 7.7–7.10)	Written Assessment, Problems 11–17 and 29–44
7e **Developing/Secure Goal** Understand and apply exponential notation. (Lessons 7.1 and 7.2)	Written Assessment, Problems 1–4, 8, 10, 17, and 28
7f **Developing/Secure Goal** Determine whether number sentences are true or false. (Lesson 7.4)	Written Assessment, Problems 17 and 18
7g **Developing/Secure Goal** Understand the function and placement of parentheses in number sentences. (Lesson 7.4)	Written Assessment, Problems 19–28
7h **Developing/Secure Goal** Compare and order integers. (Lesson 7.6)	Slate Assessment, Problem 1 Written Assessment, Problems 5–16

Alternative Assessment

In Lesson 7.11, you will find alternative assessment options on pages 562 and 563.

✦ **Play *Exponent Ball***

Students play a game that is similar to football in the United States. They roll a die twice; the first roll gives the base and the second roll gives the exponent. Then students find the value of the rolls and move on a game board. As students play the game, observe whether:

• Students know which number is the base and which is the exponent.

• Students can find the value of a number in exponential form.

• They can move for positive and negative values on the game board.

✦ **Write Number Stories to Match Number Sentences**

Students write number stories for given number sentences. As you circulate to check students work, keep these questions in mind:

• Is the story complete? Are all of the numbers in the problem used?

• Does the number story reflect understanding of parentheses?

• Does the number story show that the student understands the order of operations?

✦ *Math Masters,* p. 440

✦ Play *Name That Number*

Students combine five numbers, using addition, subtraction, multiplication, and division to equal a target number. Have students write their solutions on a sheet of paper, which you can collect and assess. As you check their papers, keep these questions in mind:

- Can the student make number sentences with all four operations, or does he or she just rely on addition and subtraction?
- Was the student able to insert parentheses correctly to make his or her number sentences?
- Is the student able to follow the correct order of operations to make his or her number sentences?
- Do all of the student's number sentences produce the correct target numbers?

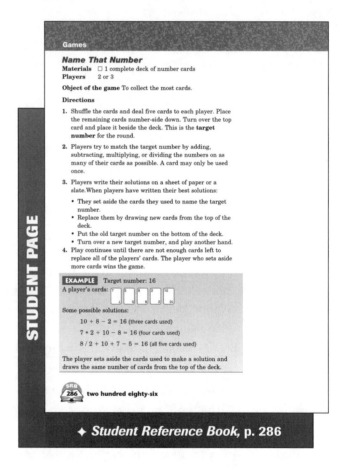

STUDENT PAGE

Games

Name That Number
Materials ☐ 1 complete deck of number cards
Players 2 or 3

Object of the game To collect the most cards.

Directions

1. Shuffle the cards and deal five cards to each player. Place the remaining cards number-side down. Turn over the top card and place it beside the deck. This is the **target number** for the round.

2. Players try to match the target number by adding, subtracting, multiplying, or dividing the numbers on as many of their cards as possible. A card may only be used once.

3. Players write their solutions on a sheet of paper or a slate. When players have written their best solutions:
   - They set aside the cards they used to name the target number.
   - Replace them by drawing new cards from the top of the deck.
   - Put the old target number on the bottom of the deck.
   - Turn over a new target number, and play another hand.

4. Play continues until there are not enough cards left to replace all of the players' cards. The player who sets aside more cards wins the game.

EXAMPLE Target number: 16
A player's cards:

Some possible solutions:

  $10 + 8 - 2 = 16$ (three cards used)

  $7 * 2 + 10 - 8 = 16$ (four cards used)

  $8 / 2 + 10 + 7 - 5 = 16$ (all five cards used)

The player sets aside the cards used to make a solution and draws the same number of cards from the top of the deck.

286 two hundred eighty-six

✦ Student Reference Book, p. 286

Unit 8
Assessment Overview

In this unit, students develop their skills with fractions. By this time, perhaps you have tried several different types of assessment strategies. Remember, as you use a balance of assessment approaches, the overall effectiveness of your assessment plan should improve. If there is still a major type of assessment, such as Ongoing, Product, or Periodic, that you haven't used, this unit might be a good time to try it.

Ongoing Assessment Opportunities

Ongoing assessment provides opportunities to observe students during regular interactions as they work independently and in groups. You can conduct ongoing assessment during teacher-guided instruction, Math Boxes sessions, mathematical mini-interviews, games, Mental Math and Reflexes sessions, strategy sharing, and slate work. The chart below provides a summary of ongoing assessment opportunities in Unit 8 as they relate to specific Unit 8 learning goals.

8a	**Beginning Goal** Use an algorithm to multiply mixed numbers. (Lesson 8.8)	Lesson 8.8, p. 824
8b	**Developing Goal** Use an algorithm to multiply fractions. (Lessons 8.5–8.7 and 8.9)	Lesson 8.6, p. 613 Lesson 8.7, p. 619
8c	**Developing Goal** Use an algorithm to subtract mixed numbers with like denominators. (Lesson 8.3)	Lesson 8.3, p. 592
8d	**Developing Goal** Find a percent of a number. (Lessons 8.9–8.11)	Lesson 8.9, p. 628
8e	**Developing/Secure Goal** Use an algorithm to add mixed numbers. (Lessons 8.2 and 8.4)	Lesson 8.2, p. 587
8f	**Developing/Secure Goal** Order and compare fractions. (Lessons 8.1, 8.2, and 8.12)	Lesson 8.1, p. 581

Product Assessment Opportunities

Math Journals, Math Boxes, Activity Sheets, *Math Masters,* math logs, and the results of Projects all provide product assessment opportunities. Here is an example of how you might use a rubric to assess a student's ability to describe population trends.

Lesson 8.11, p. 643

ENRICHMENT **Writing About Population Trends**

Most of your students should be able to suggest some reasons why the urban population became so much larger than the rural population during the 1900s, but knowledge of U.S. history will also vary. Some students may do extensive research to complete this activity. Use your own rubric, or the sample rubric below, to evaluate students' work.

Sample Rubric

Beginning (B)
The student attempts to write a percent-of problem, but teacher assistance is required. He or she writes a story that involves a percent, but it is not a percent-of type problem. The student lacks understanding of the concept. The question asked is incorrect or is missing.

Developing (D)
The student writes a percent-of problem independently. He or she writes a story that involves a percent and requires finding a percent of a given value. The question asked is appropriate. The story written involves an easy percent, such as a multiple of 10.

Secure (S)
The student writes a percent-of problem independently. He or she writes a story involving the percent of a given value. The question asked is appropriate. This story may involve a more difficult percent or the question requires calculating the list price of an item versus the discount.

Periodic Assessment Opportunities

Here is a summary of the periodic assessment opportunities that are provided in Unit 8. Refer to Lesson 8.13 for details.

Oral and Slate Assessment

In Lesson 8.13, you will find oral and slate assessment problems on pages 651 and 652.

Written Assessment

In Lesson 8.12, you will find written assessment problems on page 653 (*Math Masters,* pages 398 and 399).

See the following chart to find oral, slate, and written assessment problems that address specific learning goals.

8a	**Beginning Goal** Use an algorithm to multiply mixed numbers. (Lesson 8.8)	Written Assessment, Problems 8, 28, and 29
8b	**Developing Goal** Use an algorithm to multiply fractions. (Lessons 8.5–8.7 and 8.9)	Written Assessment, Problems 18, 26, and 37
8c	**Developing Goal** Use an algorithm to subtract mixed numbers with like denominators. (Lesson 8.3)	Written Assessment, Problems 7, 13, and 15–17
8d	**Developing Goal** Find a percent of a number. (Lessons 8.9–8.11)	Slate Assessment, Problem 3 Written Assessment, Problem 19
8e	**Developing/Secure Goal** Use an algorithm to add mixed numbers. (Lessons 8.2 and 8.4)	Written Assessment, Problems 8, 12, and 14
8f	**Developing/Secure Goal** Order and compare fractions. (Lessons 8.1, 8.2, and 8.12)	Written Assessment, Problems 5, 6, and 25
8g	**Secure Goal** Convert among fractions, decimals, and percents. (Lessons 8.8 and 8.9)	Slate Assessment, Problem 4 Written Assessment, Problems 1 and 2
8h	**Secure Goal** Convert between fractions and mixed or whole numbers. (Lessons 8.2, 8.3, and 8.8)	Oral Assessment. Problem 2 Slate Assessment, Problem 2 Written Assessment, Problems 20–23
8i	**Secure Goal** Find common denominators. (Lesson 8.1, 8.2, 8.4, and 8.12)	Slate Assessment, Problem 1 Written Assessment, Problems 3, 4, 9–12, 14, and 24

Alternative Assessment

In Lesson 8.13, you will find alternative assessment options on page 654.

✦ Percent-of Problems

This activity is intended to assess a student's skill at writing percent-of number stories. Consider the following questions:

• Is the story complete? (Is information given and a question posed?)

• Does the number story ask a question that can be answered using the information given?

• Does the number story reflect understanding of finding the percent of a number?

✦ *Math Masters*, p. 442

✦ Measure to Find Areas

Students work with a partner to measure rectangular surfaces in the room to the nearest $\frac{1}{4}$- or $\frac{1}{8}$-inch. They compute the approximate area of the surface. Use a Class Checklist or Calendar Grid to record students' progress. As students work, keep these questions in mind:

• Can the students measure to the nearest $\frac{1}{4}$- or $\frac{1}{8}$-inch accurately?

• Are the students able to use the mixed number multiplication algorithm?

✦ Play *Frac-Tac-Toe*

Use *Math Masters,* page 62, to assess students' abilities to convert between fractions, decimals, and percents. As students work with a partner to play the games, keep the following questions in mind:

• Can the student recognize a fraction equal to 0 or 1?

• Is the student able to use a calculator to find the appropriate decimal or percent?

• Is the student able to recognize that a decimal or a percent is greater than a given decimal or percent?

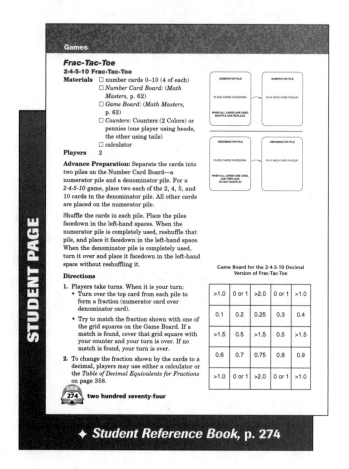

✦ *Student Reference Book,* p. 274

Unit 9
Assessment Overview

Unit 9 deals with area, volume, and coordinate graphing. Depending on the specific skill, students' ability levels for these skills might range from Developing to Secure. A good mix of ongoing assessment opportunities is suggested in the chart below for several of these learning goals. The chart on pages 64 and 65 indicates where you can find oral, written, and slate assessments to measure student progress toward these goals.

Ongoing Assessment Opportunities

Ongoing assessment provides opportunities to observe students during regular interactions as they work independently and in groups. You can conduct ongoing assessment during teacher-guided instruction, Math Boxes sessions, mathematical mini-interviews, games, Mental Math and Reflexes sessions, strategy sharing, and slate work. The chart below provides a summary of ongoing assessment opportunities in Unit 9 as they relate to specific Unit 9 learning goals.

9b **Developing/Secure Goal** Understand the concept of volume of a figure. (Lessons 9.8–9.10)	Lesson 9.10, p. 722
9c **Developing Goal** Use a formula to find the volume of prisms. (Lessons 9.8 and 9.9)	Lesson 9.9, p. 718
9d **Secure Goal** Plot ordered pairs on a one-quadrant coordinate grid. (Lessons 9.1–9.3)	Lesson 9.1, p. 672
9f **Developing/Secure Goal** Use a formula to find the area of triangles and parallelograms. (Lesson 9.6)	Lesson 9.6, p. 699
9g **Secure Goal** Understand the concept of area of a figure. (Lessons 9.4–9.6)	Lesson 9.5, p. 694

Product Assessment Opportunities

Math Journals, Math Boxes, Activity Sheets, *Math Masters,* math logs, and the results of Projects all provide product assessment opportunities. On the next page is an example of how you might use a rubric to assess a student's ability to find the volume of prisms.

Lesson 9.11, p. 728

ALTERNATIVE ASSESSMENT Plot Pictures

Most of your students should be able to create a simple
picture and plot the appropriate points using *Math
Masters*, page 138. Some students may feel more
comfortable using only a one-quadrant grid. Use your
own rubric, or the sample rubric below, to evaluate students' work.

Portfolio Ideas

Sample Rubric
Beginning (B)
The student independently draws a simple picture on the grid, but the picture only uses the first quadrant of the grid. The student plots fewer than 8 points on the grid and records the ordered pairs, but they are not given in the order in which they need to be connected to complete the drawing correctly. This student may also turn around the ordered pair, giving the *y*-axis first and the *x*-axis second.
Developing (D)
The student independently draws a simple picture on the grid that uses more than the first quadrant of the grid. The student plots at least 8 points on the grid. He or she correctly records the ordered pairs, and they are given in the order in which they need to be connected.
Secure (S)
The student independently draws a more complex picture on the four-quadrant grid, using up to 14 points. The student utilizes all four quadrants on the grid. He or she correctly records the ordered pairs, and they are given in the order in which they need to be connected.

Periodic Assessment Opportunities

Here is a summary of the periodic assessment opportunities that
are provided in Unit 9. Refer to Lesson 9.11 for details.

Oral and Slate Assessment

In Lesson 9.11, you will find oral and slate assessment problems on
pages 726 and 727.

Written Assessment

In Lesson 9.11, you will find written assessment problems on
page 728 (*Math Masters*, pages 400–402).

See the following chart to find oral, slate, and written assessment
problems that address specific learning goals.

9a	**Developing Goal** Plot ordered pairs on a four-quadrant coordinate grid. (Lesson 9.3)	Written Assessment, Problems 2–4
9b	**Developing/Secure Goal** Understand the concept of volume of a figure. (Lessons 9.8–9.10)	Oral Assessment, Problem 1 Written Assessment, Problems 14–17, and 22
9c	**Developing Goal** Use a formula to find the volume of prisms. (Lessons 9.8 and 9.9)	Written Assessment, Problems 18–21
9d	**Secure Goal** Plot ordered pairs on a one-quadrant coordinate grid. (Lessons 9.1–9.3)	Written Assessment, Problems 1, 12, and 13

9e	**Developing/Secure Goal** Identify the base and height of triangles and parallelograms. (Lessons 9.4–9.6)	Written Assessment, Problems 10 and 13
9f	**Developing/Secure Goal** Use a formula to find the area of triangles and parallelograms. (Lesson 9.6)	Written Assessment, Problems 6–9, and 13
9g	**Secure Goal** Understand the concept of area of a figure. (Lessons 9.4–9.6)	Oral Assessment, Problem 1 Written Assessment, Problems 5 and 11
9h	**Secure Goal** Use a formula to find the area of rectangles. (Lesson 9.4)	Slate Assessment, Problem 3 Written Assessment, Problem 9

Alternative Assessment

In Lesson 9.11, you will find alternative assessment options on pages 728 and 729.

✦ Plot Pictures

Students work in pairs. Each student draws a simple picture on the grid and lists the ordered pairs for points used to make the drawing. Partners exchange their lists of ordered pairs and make each other's drawings. As you evaluate the student's work, keep the following questions in mind:

- Can the student locate the ordered pairs for his or her partner's design?
- Does the student understand how to plot points in all 4 quadrants?

✦ Write Area Number Stories

Students write area number stories. As you circulate to check students' work, use a Class Checklist or Calendar Grids to record students' progress. Keep the following questions in mind:

- Does the number story ask a question that can be answered using the information given?
- Does the number story ask a question that can be answered by finding the area?

✦ Find the Volume of One Stick-On Note

Students find the volume of a single stick-on note by first finding the volume of a pad of 100 notes. As you discuss the problem with the class, keep the following questions in mind:

- Could the class come up with a reasonable estimate of the volume of one note?
- Can the students see that the volume of one note is $\frac{1}{100}$ of the volume of the pad?

✦ *Math Masters*, p. 444

Unit 10
Assessment Overview

The major topics of this unit are prealgebra concepts and skills. Depending on the specific skill, students' ability levels might range from Beginning to Secure. A good mix of ongoing assessment opportunities is suggested in the chart below for several learning goals from this unit. Oral, written, and slate assessments for these same goals are listed in the chart on pages 67 and 68.

Ongoing Assessment Opportunities

Ongoing assessment provides opportunities to observe students during regular interactions as they work independently and in groups. You can conduct ongoing assessment during teacher-guided instruction, Math Boxes sessions, mathematical mini-interviews, games, Mental Math and Reflexes sessions, strategy sharing, and slate work. The chart below provides a summary of ongoing assessment opportunities in Unit 10 as they relate to specific Unit 10 learning goals.

10a **Beginning Goal** Solve two-step pan-balance problems. (Lessons 10.2 and 10.5)	Lesson 10.2, p. 753
10c **Developing Goal** Represent rate problems as formulas, tables, and graphs. (Lessons 10.4–10.7)	Lesson 10.3, p. 760 Lesson 10.4, p. 765
10d **Developing Goal** Use formulas to find circumference and area of a circle. (Lessons 10.8 and 10.9)	Lesson 10.9, p. 795

Product Assessment Opportunities

Math Journals, Math Boxes, Activity Sheets, *Math Masters,* math logs, and the results of Projects all provide product assessment opportunities. On the next page is an example of how you might use a rubric to assess a student's ability to write rate problems.

Lesson 10.10, p. 802

ALTERNATIVE ASSESSMENT   Write Rate Number Stories

Most of your students should be able to write a simple
rate problem, but ability levels will vary. Some students
may be able to write complicated problems, others just
simple ones. Use your own rubric, or the following
sample rubric, to evaluate students' work.

Portfolio
Ideas

Sample Rubric
Beginning (B)
The student experiences difficulty starting the activity. He or she requires teacher assistance to interpret the table and plot the points on a graph for Problems 3 and 4. As a result, the graph is incorrect (does not form a straight line). The student is unable to interpret the rule (written in words) and then represent it as a number sentence.
Developing (D)
The student interprets the tables for Problems 3 and 4 by using the information to plot the points on a graph. As a result, the points plotted form a straight line. However, the student experiences difficulty interpreting the rule (written in words) and writing it as a number sentence.
Secure (S)
The student interprets the table for Problems 3 and 4 by using the information to plot the points on a graph. As a result, the points plotted form a straight line. He or she interprets the rule (written in words) by writing it as a number sentence.

Periodic Assessment Opportunities

Here is a summary of the periodic assessment opportunities that
are provided in Unit 10. Refer to Lesson 10.10 for details.

Oral and Slate Assessment

In Lesson 10.10, you will find oral and slate assessment problems
on pages 798–800.

Written Assessment

In Lesson 10.10, you will find written assessment problems on
pages 800 and 801 (*Math Masters,* pages 403–406).

See the following chart to find slate and written assessment
problems that address specific learning goals.

10a	**Beginning Goal** Solve two-step pan-balance problems. (Lessons 10.2 and 10.5)	Written Assessment, Problem 10
10b	**Developing Goal** Write algebraic expressions to represent situations. (Lessons 10.3–10.5 and 10.7)	Slate Assessment, Problems 1 and 5 Written Assessment, Problems 1–3
10c	**Developing Goal** Represent rate problems as formulas, tables, and graphs. (Lessons 10.4–10.7)	Written Assessment, Problems 4 and 5
10d	**Developing Goal** Use formulas to find circumference and area of a circle. (Lessons 10.8 and 10.9)	Written Assessment, Problems 11–14

10e **Developing Goal** Distinguish between circumference and area of a circle. (Lesson 10.9)	Written Assessment, Problems 15–17 Oral Assessment, Problem 1
10f **Developing/Secure Goal** Solve one-step pan-balance problems. (Lessons 10.1 and 10.5)	Written Assessment, Problems 6–9
10g **Developing Goal** Interpret mystery line plots and graphs. (Lesson 10.7)	Written Assessment, Problem 18

Alternative Assessment

In Lesson 10.10, you will find alternative assessment options on page 802.

✦ Write Rate Number Stories

Students work in small groups to write and exchange rate problems. As you circulate to check students' work, keep these questions in mind:

- Is the number story complete? (Is information given and a question posed?)
- Does the number story ask a question that can be answered using the information given?
- Does the number story ask a question that is answered by finding a rate?
- Does the number story show an understanding of rates?

✦ Graph Table Values

Students work with partners. One partner reads values from a table, and the other plots the ordered pairs on a grid. As you circulate to check students' work, keep these questions in mind:

- Can the students create ordered pairs from a table of values?
- Is the student plotting the points on the grid correctly?
- Can the student write a rule for his or her graph?

✦ Collect Data for Mystery Graphs

Students work in small groups. Each group collects data for one of three questions and graphs the data. Then the groups try to match the graphs to the questions. As you circulate to check students' work, keep these questions in mind:

- Did the group collect data for its question?
- Was the group able to graph its data?
- Were students able to match the graphs to the questions?

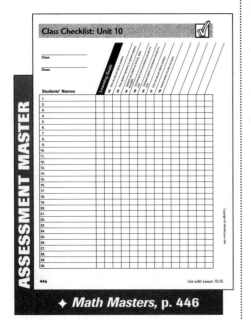

✦ *Math Masters*, p. 446

Unit 11
Assessment Overview

As you near the end of the Fifth-Grade *Everyday Mathematics* program, reflect on your success in developing a balanced assessment plan. Think about which assessment strategies worked best. Are there strategies that you did not have time to try this year, but that you would like to try next year? To help you remember them next fall, record your thoughts on the note pages in this book.

Ongoing Assessment Opportunities

Ongoing assessment provides opportunities to observe students during regular interactions as they work independently and in groups. You can conduct ongoing assessment during teacher-guided instruction, Math Boxes sessions, mathematical mini-interviews, games, Mental Math and Reflexes sessions, strategy sharing, and slate work. The chart below provides a summary of ongoing assessment opportunities in Unit 11 as they relate to specific Unit 11 learning goals.

11b	**Beginning Goal** Find the surface area of prisms. (Lesson 11.7)	Lesson 11.7, p. 851
11d	**Beginning Goal** Understand the concept of and calculate capacity. (Lesson 11.6)	Lesson 11.5, p. 840
11f	**Secure Goal** Use formulas to find the area of polygons and circles. (Lessons 11.1 and 11.4)	Lesson 11.4, p. 836
11g	**Secure Goal** Know the properties of geometric solids. (Lessons 11.1 and 11.2)	Lesson 11.1, p. 818 Lesson 11.2, p. 824

Product Assessment Opportunities

Math Journals, Math Boxes, Activity Sheets, *Math Masters,* math logs, and the results of Projects all provide product assessment opportunities. On the next page is an example of how you might use a rubric to assess a student's ability to write volume problems.

Lesson 11.8, p. 857

ALTERNATIVE ASSESSMENT Write Volume Problems

Some of your students should be able to write volume problems with little or no direction, but many might need some reminders to get started. Use your own rubric, or the following sample rubric, to evaluate students' work.

Portfolio Ideas

Sample Rubric
Beginning (B) The student attempts to independently write a number story involving the volume of an object, however he or she experiences difficulty and requires teacher assistance. As a result, the number story reflects a lack of understanding of volume, or the student may write a number story involving finding the area instead of volume.
Developing (D) The student writes a number story that involves finding the volume of an object. The number story may involve finding the volume of a simple 3-dimensional object, such as various rectangular prisms or cylinders. He or she displays an understanding of the concept of volume.
Secure (S) The student writes a number story that involves finding the volume of an object. The number story involves finding the volume of a more complex 3-dimensional figure such as a cone or pyramid. Or, the student writes a number story that reflects his or her understanding of the relationships between volumes of pyramids and prisms, and the volumes of cones and cylinders.

Periodic Assessment Opportunities

Here is a summary of the periodic assessment opportunities that are provided in Unit 11. Refer to Lesson 11.8 for details.

Oral and Slate Assessment

In Lesson 11.8, you will find oral and slate assessment problems on pages 854–856

Written Assessment

In Lesson 11.8, you will find written assessment problems on page 856 (*Math Masters*, pages 407–409).

See the following chart to find oral, slate, and written assessment problems that address specific learning goals.

11a	**Beginning Goal** Understand the relationship between the volume of pyramids and prisms and the volume of cones and cylinders. (Lesson 11.4)	Written Assessment, Problems 15 and 18
11b	**Beginning Goal** Find the surface area of prisms. (Lesson 11.7)	Written Assessment, Problems 8 and 9
11c	**Beginning Goal** Understand how to find the surface area of cylinders. (Lesson 11.7)	Written Assessment, Problem 14
11d	**Beginning Goal** Understand the concept of and calculate capacity. (Lesson 11.6)	Oral Assessment, Problem 1 Written Assessment, Problems 19 and 20

	Developing/Secure Goal Use formulas to find the volume of prisms and cylinders. (Lesson 11.3)	Written Assessment, Problems 6–7, 10–11, 13, 16–17, and 19–20
11e		
11f	Secure Goal Use formulas to find the area of polygons and circles. (Lessons 11.1 and 11.4)	Slate Assessment, Problem 3 Written Assessment, Problems 5 and 12
11g	Secure Goal Know the properties of geometric solids. (Lessons 11.1 and 11.2)	Oral Assessment, Problem 2 Written Assessment, Problems 1–4

Alternative Assessment

In Lesson 11.8, you will find alternative assessment options on page 857.

✦ Write Volume Problems

Students work in small groups as they write and exchange volume problems. As you circulate to check students' work, keep these questions in mind:

- Is the number story complete? (Is information given and a question posed?)
- Does the number story ask a question that can be answered using the information given?
- Does the number story ask a question that is answered by finding the volume?
- Does the number story show an understanding of volume? Did the group confuse volume with surface area?

✦ Play *3-D Shape Sort*

In this game, students draw property cards and take the 3-D shape cards with that property. As you observe students playing the game, use a Class Checklist or Calendar Grids to record students' progress. Keep the following questions in mind:

- Does the student quickly recognize a 3-D shape with the given property?
- Does the student recognize all 3-D shapes that fit?
- Can the student rule out 3-D shapes that do not have the property?

✦ *Math Masters,* p. 448

Unit 12
Assessment Overview

Looking back over the Fifth-Grade *Everyday Mathematics* program, have you been able to establish a balance of Ongoing, Product, and Periodic Assessment strategies? Have your strategies included keeping anecdotal records based on observations of students' progress, as well as the use of written assessments? This might be a good time to evaluate your assessment strategies and think of what approaches you might consider for next year.

Ongoing Assessment Opportunities

Ongoing assessment provides opportunities to observe students during regular interactions as they work independently and in groups. You can conduct ongoing assessment during teacher-guided instruction, Math Boxes sessions, mathematical mini-interviews, games, Mental Math and Reflexes sessions, strategy sharing, and slate work. The chart below provides a summary of ongoing assessment opportunities in Unit 12 as they relate to specific Unit 12 learning goals.

12a	**Beginning Goal** Understand and use tree diagrams to solve problems. (Lesson 12.2)	Lesson 12.2, p. 880
12d	**Developing Goal** Find the greatest common factor of two numbers. (Lesson 12.1)	Lesson 12.1, pp. 873
12f	**Developing/Secure Goal** Solve ratio and rate number stories. (Lessons 12.1, 12.3–12.8)	Lesson 12.4, p. 890 Lesson 12.8, p. 911

Product Assessment Opportunities

Math Journals, Math Boxes, Activity Sheets, *Math Masters,* math logs, and the results of Projects all provide product assessment opportunities. On the next page is an example of how you might use a rubric to assess a student's ability to make tree diagrams.

Lesson 12.2, p. 881

EXTRA PRACTICE **Making Tree Diagrams**

Some of your students should be capable of independently using tree diagrams, but ability levels will vary. Some students will be able to apply the Multiplication Counting Principle, while others will need further opportunities to build understanding. Use your own rubric, or the following sample rubric, to evaluate students' work.

> **Portfolio Ideas**

Sample Rubric
Beginning (B) The student attempts to solve the problem by using a tree diagram. However, the student requires teacher assistance in setting up the diagram. His or her tree diagram does not represent the possible outcomes for the situation. As a result, the answer is incorrect.
Developing (D) The student attempts to solve the problem independently. The tree diagram is set up correctly to represent the possible outcomes for the situation. The student may encounter difficulties interpreting the tree diagram once it is completed.
Secure (S) The student solves the problem independently. The tree diagram drawn represents the possible outcomes of the situation. As a result, the diagram reflects a correct solution. The student also applies the Multiplication Counting Principal.

Periodic Assessment Opportunities

Here is a summary of the periodic assessment opportunities that are provided in Unit 12. Refer to Lesson 12.10 for details.

Oral and Slate Assessment

In Lesson 12.10, you will find oral and slate assessment problems on pages 919–921.

Written Assessment

In Lesson 12.10, you will find written assessment problems on page 921 (*Math Masters,* pages 410–413).

See the following chart to find oral, slate, and written assessment problems that address specific learning goals.

12a **Beginning Goal** Understand and use tree diagrams to solve problems. (Lesson 12.2)	Written Assessment, Problem 9
12b **Beginning Goal** Compute the probability of outcomes when choices are equally likely. (Lesson 12.2)	Written Assessment, Problem 10
12c **Beginning/Developing Goal** Use the Multiplication Counting Principle to find the total number of possible outcomes of a sequence of choices. (Lesson 12.2)	Slate Assessment, Problem 4 Written Assessment, Problem 9
12d **Developing Goal** Find the greatest common factor of two numbers. (Lesson 12.1)	Written Assessment, Problem 4

12e **Developing Goal** Find the least common multiple of two numbers. (Lesson 12.1)	Slate Assessment, Problem 3 Written Assessment, 　Problems 5, 6–8, and 11
12f **Developing/Secure Goal** Solve ratio and rate number stories. (Lessons 12.1, 12.3–12.5, 12.7, and 12.8)	Oral Assessment, Problem 2 Written Assessment, 　Problems 12–20
12g **Secure Goal** Find the factors of numbers. (Lessons 12.1 and 12.3–12.8)	Oral Assessment, Problem 1 Slate Assessment, Problem 1 Written Assessment, 　Problems 1, 2, 6–8, and 11
12h **Secure Goal** Find the prime factorizations of numbers. (Lesson 12.1)	Written Assessment, 　Problems 1–3

Alternative Assessment

In Lesson 12.10, you will find alternative assessment options on page 922.

✦ Write Ratio Number Stories

Students work in small groups. They write and exchange ratio problems. This activity will help you assess how well students understand ratios. As you circulate to check students' work, keep these questions in mind:

Portfolio Ideas

- Is the number story complete? (Is information given and a question posed?)
- Does the number story ask a question that can be answered using the information given?
- Does the number story ask a question that is answered by finding a ratio?
- Does the number story show an understanding of ratio?

✦ Play *Spoon Scramble*

Students make their own set of cards like the ones on *Math Masters,* page 174. They play the game with a partner. As students play the game, keep these questions in mind:

- Can the student recognize equivalent ratios expressed in different ways?
- Can the student express equivalent ratios in different ways?

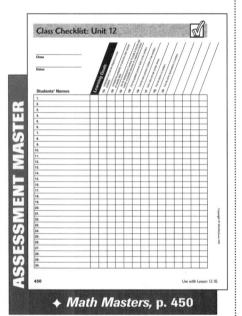

ASSESSMENT MASTER

Class Checklist: Unit 12

Class

Dates

Learning Goals

Students' Names

450　　　　　Use with Lesson 12.10.

✦ *Math Masters,* p. 450

Assessment Masters

How to Use the Masters

NOTE: This page provides a brief summary of how the general Assessment Masters may be used. The uses of these masters are described in more detail near the front of this book on pages 3–30.

The *Assessment Handbook* contains reduced versions of all of the Assessment Masters found in your *Math Masters* book. You can use these reduced pages to assist you in developing your assessment plan. The following general masters may be adapted to suit your needs; however, the suggestions below may be helpful.

Use the **List of Assessment Sources** to keep track of the sources that you are currently using. As you plan your assessment, aim for the balance of techniques that will meet your students' needs.

On the **Individual Profile of Progress**

• Copy the Learning Goals from the Review and Assessment Lesson at the end of each unit. (See the *Teacher's Lesson Guide.*)

• Make as many copies of the form as you need for each student in your class.

• Keep track of each student's progress on each unit's skills and concepts using this form.

• Check whether each student is Beginning, Developing, or Secure in each of the content areas.

• You may alternatively wish to use the **Class Checklist.**

Make several copies of the **Class Progress Indicator.** Use one page for each mathematical topic being assessed. Fill in the topic you wish to assess under the chart heading, and then write each student's name in the appropriate box, indicating whether he or she is Beginning, Developing, or Secure.

All of the other forms are to be passed out to students. Use the **Interest Inventories** to find out how students feel about mathematics. Their frank responses can be a useful planning tool for you. The **math log** forms can also provide insight into how comfortable students feel with the math content and, therefore, may also be useful planning tools. There are three versions of math logs provided: a Weekly Math Log, a generic all-purpose Math Log, and a more specific Number-Story Math Log. Both **Self-Assessment** forms should be used as attachments to portfolio items. After students have chosen the work they wish to include in their portfolios, have them reflect on their choices, using these forms.

Name   Date   Time

Unit 1 Checking Progress

1. Mr. Martin has 24 tulip bulbs. He wants to plant them in a rectangular array consisting of *at least* 2 rows with *at least* 2 tulips in each row. On the grid at the right, draw three possible arrays.

2. Is 24 an even or an odd number? **even**

3. List all the factors of 24.
   1, 2, 3, 4, 6, 8, 12, 24

4. Is 24 a prime or a composite number? **composite**

   How can you tell? **Sample answer: 24 has factors other than 1 and itself, so it is a composite number.**

5. Circle the factors in Problem 3 that are prime numbers.

6. Write the prime factorization for 24.
   2 * 2 * 2 * 3

7. Write the prime factorization of 24 using exponents.
   2³ * 3

8. Fill in the missing numbers.

   a. 7² = **49**   b. 9² = **81**   c. **36** = 6²

   d. **5**² = 25   e. **10**² = 100   f. 8 * 8 = **8²**

Name   Date   Time

Unit 1 Checking Progress (cont.)

9. Pretend that you are playing *Factor Captor* on the number grid at the right. The crossed-out numbers have already been picked. Which number would you choose next?

   Answers vary.

   Why? **Sample answer: I would choose 19. There are no factors of 19 my opponent can choose.**

10. If you chose 28 on the grid in Problem 9, what numbers would your opponent be able to capture? **2, 4, and 14**

11. Name a number between 200 and 300 that is divisible by 3 but not by 2.
    Sample answers: 231, 285

12. Name a number between 200 and 300 that is divisible by 2, 3, and 5.
    Sample answers: 210, 240, 270

13. At the right is a calendar for a month. Use the following clues to figure out on what date the Bret Harte School won its last basketball game.

    • The date is not an even number.
    • The date is not a square number.
    • The date is not a prime number.
    • The date is a multiple of 5.

    On what day of the month did the school win its last basketball game? **15**

14. Is 231 a prime or a composite number? **composite**

    Explain your answer. **Sample answer: 231 is a composite number because it has another factor that is not 1 or 231. 3 is a factor of 231 because 2 + 3 + 1 = 6, and 6 is divisible by 3.**

Name   Date   Time

Unit 2 Checking Progress

Solve at least one problem using the partial-sums addition method and at least one problem using the trade-first subtraction method. Use any method you want to solve the rest of the problems. Show your work.

1. $734 + 893 = \underline{1{,}627}$

2. $24.7 + 103.9 = \underline{128.6}$

3. $\underline{134.28} = 58.2 + 76.08$

4. $692 - 348 = \underline{344}$

5. $150.4 - 63.7 = \underline{86.7}$

6. $\underline{14.59} = 28.3 - 13.71$

Use with Lesson 2.11.

381

© 2002 Everyday Learning Corporation

Name   Date   Time

Unit 2 Checking Progress (cont.)

Round to the nearest ...

7. hundred.
   a. 84 $\underline{100}$
   b. 1,659 $\underline{1{,}700}$
   c. 46,310 $\underline{46{,}300}$

8. one.
   a. 243.6 $\underline{244}$
   b. 170.3 $\underline{170}$
   c. 1,419.78 $\underline{1{,}420}$

9. tenth.
   a. 604.37 $\underline{604.4}$
   b. 291.06 $\underline{291.1}$
   c. 12.74 $\underline{12.7}$

10. ten.
    a. 493 $\underline{490}$
    b. 1,508 $\underline{1{,}510}$
    c. 124.63 $\underline{120}$

11. Write the number that has
    6 in the ones place,
    4 in the thousands place,
    7 in the ten-thousands place,
    2 in the tenths place,
    and 5 in all of the remaining places.
    $\underline{7 \; 4 \, , \, 5 \; 5 \; 6 \, . \, 2 \; 5 \; 5}$

12. Identify the errors in the following problems and correct them.

    a.
    ```
      28
    ×  46
      80   — Should be 800
     120
     320
    + 48   — Should be
     488     1,288
    ```

    b. (lattice multiplication grid, 3 6 across top, 2 on right)

    ```
       3   6
     0/ 0/    2
      6   2
     0/ 1/    5
      6   0   3
    ```
    Should be 1
    Should be 3
    Should be 0
    Should be 0

    Should be 9 – 4
    Should be 0 – 7

13. Choose one of the problems above and explain why making a quick estimate of the answer before solving the problem would be helpful.
    Sample answer: By making an estimate, you would know that your answer was wrong because the estimate and the answer would be very different.

382

Use with Lesson 2.11.

Unit 2 Checking Progress (cont.)

For each problem, make a magnitude estimate. Circle the appropriate box.
Then solve the problem. Show your work.

14. 64 * 83 = __5,312__

| 10s | 100s | 1,000s | 10,000s |

15. 5 * 209 = __1,045__

| 10s | 100s | 1,000s | 10,000s |

16. 12.2 * 1.56 = __19.032__

| 10s | 100s | 1,000s | 10,000s |

17. 25 * 15.3 = __382.5__

| 10s | 100s | 1,000s | 10,000s |

18. Elise had the following scores on her spelling tests: 78, 84, 94, 94, 98, 62, 96, 89, 94, 92.
For this set of data, find …

a. the maximum __98__   **b.** the minimum __62__

c. the range __36__   **d.** the mode __94__   **e.** the median __92__

19. Caitlin's great-grandmother was born in 1919. Her family had a big party for
her on her 75th birthday. There were 52 family members at the party. In
what year did they have the party?

a. List the numbers needed to solve the problem. __1919 and 75__

b. Describe what you want to find. __The year of the birthday party__

c. Open sentence: __1919 + 75 = p__

d. Solution: __1994__   **e.** Answer: __1994__

Unit 3 Checking Progress

Find the missing angle measures without measuring.

1.

m∠DBC = __50__ °

2.

m∠E = __100__ °

3.

Each angle at
point *H* has a
measure of __120__ °.

Measure each angle below with a protractor. Then fill in an oval to tell what kind
of angle it is.

4.

m∠FOG = __105__ °

○ acute
● obtuse
○ adjacent
○ right

5.

m∠CAP = __90__ °

○ acute
○ obtuse
○ adjacent
● right

6.

m∠T = __65__ °

● acute
○ obtuse
○ adjacent
○ right

7. Explain what a reflex angle is. __A reflex angle is an angle that is greater
than 180°.__

Name   Date   Time

Unit 3 Checking Progress (cont.)

15. In the space below, use the pattern-block shapes on your Geometry Template to make a pattern that tessellates. (The pattern-block shapes are marked PB.) **Sample answers:**

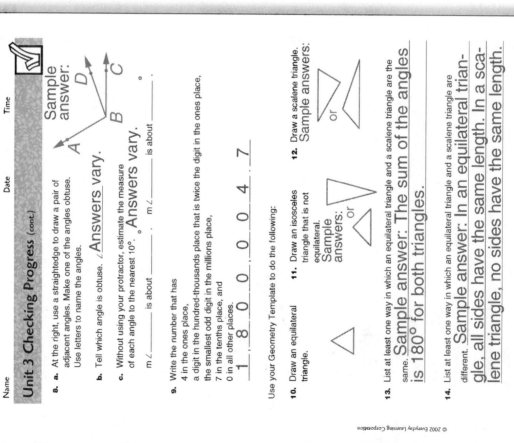

16. Explain why your pattern above is a tessellation.
Sample answer: The shapes create a pattern in which there are no gaps or overlaps.

For each polygon below, fill in the ovals next to the true statements.

17.

- ● This polygon is a quadrangle.
- ● At least two sides are parallel.
- ● At least two angles are congruent.
- ○ This is a regular polygon.

18.

- ○ This polygon is a quadrangle.
- ● At least two sides are parallel.
- ○ At least one angle is acute.
- ● At least two angles are congruent.
- ● This is a regular polygon.

© 2002 Everyday Learning Corporation

Use with Lesson 3.11.

Name   Date   Time

Unit 3 Checking Progress (cont.)

8. a. At the right, use a straightedge to draw a pair of adjacent angles. Make one of the angles obtuse. Use letters to name the angles. **Sample answer:** ∠A, ∠B, ∠C, ∠D

b. Tell which angle is obtuse. ∠ _____ **Answers vary.**

c. Without using your protractor, estimate the measure of each angle to the nearest 10°. **Answers vary.**

m∠ _____ is about _____°. m∠ _____ is about _____°.

9. Write the number that has
4 in the ones place,
a digit in the hundred-thousands place that is twice the digit in the ones place,
the smallest odd digit in the millions place,
7 in the tenths place, and
0 in all other places.

1 , 8 0 0 , 0 0 4 . 7

Use your Geometry Template to do the following:

10. Draw an equilateral triangle.

11. Draw an isosceles triangle that is not equilateral.
Sample answers: ____ or ____

12. Draw a scalene triangle.
Sample answers: ____ or ____

13. List at least one way in which an equilateral triangle and a scalene triangle are the same. **Sample answer: The sum of the angles is 180° for both triangles.**

14. List at least one way in which an equilateral triangle and a scalene triangle are different. **Sample answer: In an equilateral triangle, all sides have the same length. In a scalene triangle, no sides have the same length.**

© 2002 Everyday Learning Corporation

Use with Lesson 3.11.

Unit 4 Checking Progress

Use a "friendly number" strategy to solve these problems mentally.

1. 84 divided by 6 equals __14__.
   __60 and 24__
   (friendly parts for 84)

2. 104 divided by 8 equals __13__.
   __80 and 24__
   (friendly parts for 104)

Sample answers provided in Problems 1 and 2 for friendly parts of numbers.

Solve. Show your work.

3. $126 / 6 =$ __21__

4. $9 *$ __27__ $= 243$

5. $703 \div 14 \rightarrow$ __50 R3__

6. $482 \div 34 \rightarrow$ __14 R6__

Circle your magnitude estimate. Then solve.

7. 5)88.5   __17.7__

   [0.1s] [1s] (10s) [100s]

8. 14)2.94   __0.21__

   (0.1s) [1s] [10s] [100s]

Use with Lesson 4.7.

387

Unit 4 Checking Progress (cont.)

In Problems 9 and 10:
- Write a number sentence to represent the number story.
- Use a division algorithm to solve the problem.
- Decide what to do about the remainder.
- Tell why you did what you did about the remainder.

9. Tammy has 130 photographs. She can tape 8 photos onto each page of her photo album. How many pages will she need to tape all of her photos in the album?
   Number sentence: $130 \div 8 = P$ or $8 * P = 130$ Solution: __17__ pages

   What does the remainder represent? The 2 photographs remaining after 16 pages have been completely filled

   What did you do about the remainder? Circle the answer.
   Ignored it.   Reported it as a fraction or decimal.   (Rounded the answer up.)

10. For a relay race, the gym teacher divided the class into 4 teams with an equal number of students on each team. There were 30 students in the class. Extra students didn't race. How many members were on each team?
    Number sentence: $30 \div 4 = t$ or $4 * t = 30$ Solution: __7__ members

    What does the remainder represent? The 2 students who didn't race

    What did you do about the remainder? Circle the answer.
    (Ignored it.)   Reported it as a fraction or decimal.   Rounded the answer up.

In Problems 11 and 12:
- Find the value of x in the first number sentence.
- Use this value to complete the second number sentence.

11. $x = 100 - 95$; $x^2 =$ __25__

12. $x = \frac{1}{2}$ of a dozen; $30 * x =$ __180__

13. Write an open sentence you can use to solve the number story below. Then solve the number story.
    Four friends rented a car. The total rental cost was $150, including tax. The friends split the cost evenly. How much did each friend contribute?
    Number sentence: $150 \div 4 = c$ or $4 * c = 150$ Solution: $ __37.50__

388

Use with Lesson 4.7.

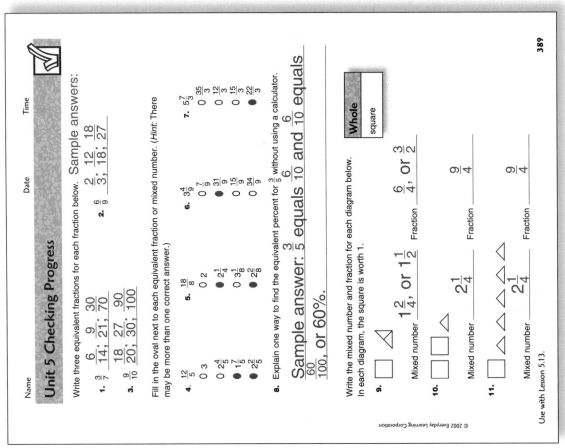

Name _____ Date _____ Time _____

Unit 5 Checking Progress

Write three equivalent fractions for each fraction below. Sample answers:

1. $\frac{3}{7}$ = $\frac{6}{14}$, $\frac{9}{21}$, $\frac{30}{70}$

2. $\frac{6}{9}$ = $\frac{2}{3}$, $\frac{12}{18}$, $\frac{18}{27}$

3. $\frac{9}{10}$ = $\frac{18}{20}$, $\frac{27}{30}$, $\frac{90}{100}$

Fill in the oval next to each equivalent fraction or mixed number. (*Hint*: There may be more than one correct answer.)

4. $\frac{12}{5}$
○ 3
○ $2\frac{4}{5}$
● $1\frac{7}{5}$
● $2\frac{2}{5}$

5. $\frac{18}{8}$
○ 2
● $2\frac{1}{4}$
○ $3\frac{1}{8}$
● $2\frac{2}{8}$

6. $\frac{34}{9}$
○ $\frac{7}{9}$
● $\frac{31}{9}$
○ $\frac{15}{9}$
○ $\frac{34}{9}$

7. $5\frac{7}{3}$
○ $\frac{35}{3}$
○ $\frac{12}{3}$
○ $\frac{15}{3}$
● $\frac{22}{3}$

8. Explain one way to find the equivalent percent for $\frac{3}{5}$ without using a calculator.
Sample answer: $\frac{3}{5}$ equals $\frac{6}{10}$ and $\frac{6}{10}$ equals $\frac{60}{100}$, or 60%.

Write the mixed number and fraction for each diagram below. In each diagram, the square is worth 1.

Whole
square

9. (triangle)
Mixed number $1\frac{1}{4}$, or $1\frac{1}{2}$
Fraction $\frac{6}{4}$, or $\frac{3}{2}$

10. (square + triangle)
Mixed number $2\frac{1}{4}$
Fraction $\frac{9}{4}$

11. (square + triangles)
Mixed number $2\frac{1}{4}$
Fraction $\frac{9}{4}$

Use with Lesson 5.13.

389

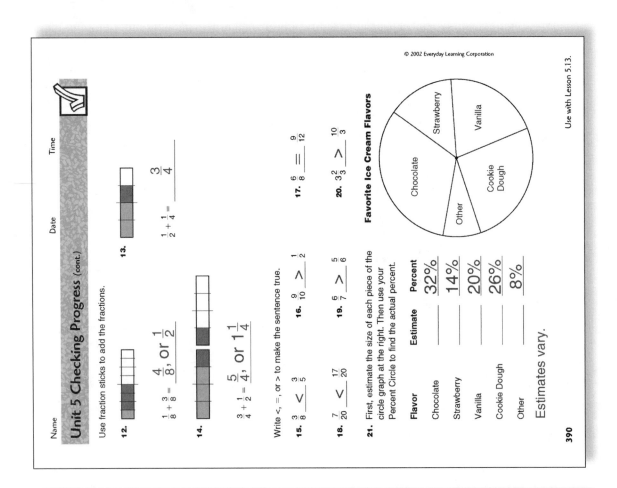

Name _____ Date _____ Time _____

Unit 5 Checking Progress (cont.)

Use fraction sticks to add the fractions.

12. [fraction stick]
$\frac{1}{8} + \frac{3}{8} = \frac{4}{8}$, or $\frac{1}{2}$

13. [fraction stick]
$\frac{1}{2} + \frac{1}{4} = \frac{3}{4}$

14. [fraction stick]
$\frac{3}{4} + \frac{1}{2} = \frac{5}{4}$, or $1\frac{1}{4}$

Write <, =, or > to make the sentence true.

15. $\frac{3}{8}$ < $\frac{3}{5}$

16. $\frac{9}{10}$ > $\frac{1}{2}$

17. $\frac{6}{8}$ = $\frac{9}{12}$

18. $\frac{7}{20}$ < $\frac{17}{20}$

19. $\frac{6}{7}$ > $\frac{5}{6}$

20. $3\frac{2}{3}$ > $\frac{10}{3}$

21. First, estimate the size of each piece of the circle graph at the right. Then use your Percent Circle to find the actual percent.

Favorite Ice Cream Flavors

Flavor	Estimate	Percent
Chocolate		32%
Strawberry		14%
Vanilla		20%
Cookie Dough		26%
Other		8%

Estimates vary.

Use with Lesson 5.13.

390

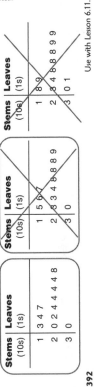

Name   Date   Time

Unit 6 Checking Progress

Fill in the ovals to match the words with their definitions.

1. Median
- ○ smallest value
- ○ largest value
- ○ most frequent value
- ● middle value

2. Maximum
- ○ smallest value
- ● largest value
- ○ most frequent value
- ○ middle value

3. Mode
- ○ smallest value
- ○ largest value
- ● most frequent value
- ○ middle value

4. Minimum
- ● smallest value
- ○ largest value
- ○ most frequent value
- ○ middle value

5. Sonia asked seven girls in her fifth grade class how many CDs they own. Here are the results of her survey:

2   0   6   5   7   5   1

a. What was the median number of CDs owned?   __5 CDs__

b. Sonia concluded: *The typical fifth grader owns about 5 CDs.*
Do you agree with her conclusion? __Answers vary.__
Explain. __Answers vary.__

c. Describe two ways Sonia could improve her survey. __Sample answer:__
__Ask more students. Ask boys and girls.__

6. Explain one way to rename $\frac{3}{5}$ as a percent without using a calculator.
__Sample answer: Rewrite $\frac{3}{5}$ as $\frac{6}{10}$, or $\frac{60}{100}$;__
__$\frac{6}{10}$ or $\frac{60}{100} = 60\%$, so $\frac{3}{5} = 60\%$.__

7. Circle each stem-and-leaf plot with a median of 24. Put an X through each stem-and-leaf plot with a mode of 28. (There may be more than one.)

Stems (10s)	Leaves (1s)
1	3 4 7
2	0 2 4 4 4 4 8
3	3 0

Stems (10s)	Leaves (1s)
1	5 6 7
2	3 4 8 8 8 9
3	0

Stems (10s)	Leaves (1s)
1	8 9
2	3 4 8 8 8 9 9
3	0 1

Use with Lesson 6.11.

392

Name   Date   Time

Unit 5 Checking Progress (cont.)

22. Why is it helpful to make an estimate before finding the size of a piece of a circle graph? __Answers vary.__

A survey reported favorite types of books for fifth graders. The results of the survey were as follows:

38% Adventure books   30% Mystery books   22% Humor books   10% Other

23. Make a circle graph for this data on the circle below. Use your Percent Circle.

Favorite Books

(circle graph with sections: Adventure, Mystery, Humor, Other)

24. If 100 students answered the survey, how many of them chose "adventures"? __38__

25. If 10 students answered the survey, how many of them chose "other"? __1__

26. If 50 students answered the survey, how many of them chose "mysteries"? __15__

Use with Lesson 5.13.

391

Left page (393)

Name   Date   Time

Unit 6 Checking Progress (cont.)

8. One survey reported favorite types of books for fifth graders. The results of the survey were as follows:

adventure books: 38%
mystery books: 30%
comedies: 22%
other: 10%

a. Circle the bar graph that best represents the survey results.

b. If 100 students answered the survey, how many of them chose "adventures"? __38__
c. If 10 students answered the survey, how many of them chose "other"? __1__
d. If 50 students answered the survey, how many of them chose "mysteries"? __15__
e. If you were trying to decide what kinds of books to buy for the library in your town, how many fifth graders would you interview? __Answers vary.__

Explain why you chose that number. __Answers vary.__

Solve.

9. $\frac{4}{5} + \frac{2}{5} = \frac{6}{5}$, or $1\frac{1}{5}$

10. $1 - \frac{3}{4} = \frac{1}{4}$

11. $\frac{5}{8} - \frac{3}{8} = \frac{2}{8}$, $= \frac{1}{4}$

12. $\frac{9}{16} + \frac{2}{8} = \frac{13}{16}$

13. $\begin{array}{r} \frac{7}{8} \\ -\frac{1}{2} \\ \hline \frac{3}{8} \end{array}$

14. $\begin{array}{r} \frac{2}{3} \\ +\frac{2}{5} \\ \hline 1\frac{1}{15} \end{array}$

15. $\begin{array}{r} \frac{5}{6} \\ -\frac{3}{8} \\ \hline \frac{11}{24} \end{array}$

16. $\begin{array}{r} \frac{2}{3} \\ +\frac{3}{4} \\ \hline 1\frac{5}{12} \end{array}$

17. a. Use your ruler to draw a line segment that is $2\frac{3}{8}$ inches long.
b. If you erased $\frac{3}{4}$ inch from this line segment, how long would it be? __$1\frac{5}{8}$ in.__
c. If you drew a line segment twice as long as the original line segment, how long would it be? __$4\frac{6}{8}$ in., or $4\frac{3}{4}$ in.__

18. Circle the fraction pair that is represented in the drawing below.

$\frac{2}{5}$ and $\frac{3}{5}$ $\frac{5}{3}$ and $\frac{9}{5}$

$\boxed{\frac{2}{3} \text{ and } \frac{3}{4}}$ $\frac{4}{15}$ and $\frac{2}{15}$

Use with Lesson 6.11.

393

Right page (394)

Name   Date   Time

Unit 6 Checking Progress (cont.)

19. Write a pair of fractions with common denominators for the pictures in Problem 18. $\frac{8}{12}$ $\frac{9}{12}$

20. Explain how you would use the multiplication rule to find common denominators for the fraction pair you circled in Problem 18.
__Sample answer: Multiply the denominators, 3 and 4, to get the common denominator of 12.__

21. David was writing a report on sleep and dreams. He gave a survey to the 21 students in his class. The following were three of the questions:

A. About how many hours do you sleep each night?
B. About how many dreams do you remember having in an average week?
C. What time do you usually get up on a school day?

The graphs below show the answers to two of these questions. Match the questions with their graphs. (Write A, B, or C under each graph.)

__A__   __B__

22. Martha's class was estimating the number of jellybeans in a jar. They made the following estimates:

128, 126, 135, 139, 132, 130, 145, 147, 155, 120, 191, 135, 145, 135, 137, 158

a. Explain the mistake in the stem-and-leaf plot for the jellybean estimates.
__Sample answer: 135 appears only once, and it should appear 3 times. 145 appears once; it should appear 2 times.__

Stems (10s)	Leaves (1s)
12	8 6 0
13	5 9 2 0 7 5 5
14	5 7 5
15	5 8
19	1

b. Correct the stem-and-leaf plot at the right.

Use with Lesson 6.11.

394

Unit 7 Checking Progress

Name _____ Date _____ Time _____

Write each number in standard notation and in number-and-word notation.

Number	Standard Notation	Number-and-Word Notation
1. 10^5	100,000	100 thousand
2. 10^9	1,000,000,000	1 billion
3. $6 * 10^7$	60,000,000	60 million
4. $3.2 * 10^6$	3,200,000	3 million 200 thousand

Write >, <, or =.

5. $-4 \;\underline{<}\; 3$

6. $-12 \;\underline{<}\; -10$

7. $37 \;\underline{>}\; -42$

8. $10^2 \;\underline{>}\; -200$

9. $\frac{3}{8} \;\underline{>}\; -1$

10. $9^2 \;\underline{<}\; 6^3$

11. $-8 \;\underline{=}\; 5 + (-13)$

12. $-4 + (-4) \;\underline{>}\; -11$

13. $12 + (-6) \;\underline{>}\; -15$

14. $-3 + (-3) \;\underline{=}\; -6$

15. $7 \;\underline{<}\; -1 - (-10)$

16. $24 / 3 \;\underline{<}\; 6 - (-7)$

17. Some of the expressions below are not number sentences. Cross them out. Then circle the number sentences that are true.

$\left(14 + (-25) > -50\right)$

$6^2 = 2^6$

$11 \times 11 \times 11 = 33^3$

2 * 10³ ~~(crossed out)~~

$-21 - (-39) = 60$

$\left(38 < 7^2 - (-20)\right)$

$\left(\dfrac{3}{4} + \dfrac{3}{4} > 1\right)$

19 ~~(crossed out)~~

$\left(-5 = 20 + (-25)\right)$

18. Explain why the expressions you crossed out in Problem 17 are not number sentences.

Sample answer: The expressions do not have an equals sign or an inequality sign.

Unit 7 Checking Progress (cont.)

Name _____ Date _____ Time _____

19. Draw a line from each story to the number model that matches.

a. Sandy baked 4 trays of chocolate-chip cookies with one dozen on each tray. She and her brother ate 6 of the cookies while they were still warm. ——— $4 * 12 - 6$

$6 * 12 - 4$

b. Charlie baked 4 trays of chocolate-chip cookies. He started with one dozen on each tray, but then his mom came and removed 6 cookies from each tray to send to Charlie's grandmother. $6 * (12 - 4)$

$4 * (12 - 6)$

20. Explain your answers to Problem 19.

Sample answers: For Problem a, 4 trays with 12 cookies on each tray is $4 * 12$. Eating 6 cookies subtracts 6, leaving $4 * 12 - 6$.

For Problem b, each tray had 12 cookies. 6 cookies were removed from each tray, leaving $12 - 6$ cookies per tray. There were 4 trays, so $4 * (12 - 6)$ cookies were left.

Insert parentheses when necessary to make the number sentences true. (Because of the rules of order of operations, some of the problems do not need parentheses.)

21. $9 + 2 * 5 = 19$

22. $(9 + 2) * 5 = 55$

23. $12 + 8 \div 2 = 16$

24. $(12 + 8) \div 2 = 10$

25. $(-8 + 43) \div 5 = 7$

26. $12 + 4 \div 8 = 12\frac{1}{2}$

27. $(-3 + 5) * (2 - (-6)) = 16$

28. $4^2 + ((-3) - (-5)) * 2 = 20$

Unit 7 Checking Progress (cont.)

Use your $\boxed{+}$ and $\boxed{-}$ counters.

29. Draw a picture that shows an account with a balance of −$6.

Sample answer: $\boxed{-}$ $\boxed{-}$ $\boxed{-}$ $\boxed{-}$ $\boxed{-}$ $\boxed{-}$

30. Draw a picture that shows a balance of $8, using exactly 10 counters.

$\boxed{+}$ $\boxed{+}$ $\boxed{+}$ $\boxed{+}$ $\boxed{+}$
$\boxed{+}$ $\boxed{+}$ $\boxed{+}$ $\boxed{-}$ $\boxed{-}$

31. What is your balance if you have the same number of $\boxed{+}$ and $\boxed{-}$ counters? **$0**

There are 15 $\boxed{+}$ and 10 $\boxed{-}$ counters in a container.

32. What is the balance in the container? **5 $\boxed{+}$**

33. How many $\boxed{-}$ counters do you
need to add to add to get a negative balance? **6**

34. What will be the new balance if you remove
6 $\boxed{-}$ counters from the original balance? **11 $\boxed{+}$**

35. What will be the new balance if you ...

a. remove 7 $\boxed{-}$ counters from the original balance? **12 $\boxed{+}$**

b. add 3 $\boxed{-}$ counters to the original balance? **2 $\boxed{+}$**

Solve. You may use your $\boxed{+}$ and $\boxed{-}$ counters or your slide rule to help you.

36. $6 + (-8) =$ **−2**

37. $(-9) + (-6) =$ **−15**

38. $16 + (-5) =$ **11**

39. $(-7) + 13 =$ **6**

40. $(-14) - 3 =$ **−17**

41. $(-8) - (-5) =$ **−3**

42. $6 - (-11) =$ 17

43. $17 - 20 =$ **−3**

44. Kerri is playing a game. She is 8 points "in the hole." (She has −8 points.)

a. She gets 12 points on her next turn. What is her score now? **+4 points**

b. If she loses 12 points instead, what will her score be? **−20 points**

Unit 8 Checking Progress

© 2002 Everyday Learning Corporation

Write each fraction as a decimal and a percent.

1. $\frac{7}{10}$ **0.7; 70%**

2. $\frac{8}{25}$ **0.32; 32%**

3. What is a common denominator for $\frac{1}{4}$ and $\frac{4}{7}$? **28**

4. Explain how you found the common denominator in Problem 3.
**Sample answer: I multiplied the two denominators:
4 * 7 = 28.**

5. Is $\frac{13}{25}$ greater than or less than $\frac{1}{2}$? **Greater than**

6. Explain how you decided on your answer for Problem 5.
Sample answer: $\frac{13}{25} = \frac{26}{50}$. Since $\frac{1}{2} = \frac{25}{50}$, $\frac{13}{25}$ is greater than $\frac{1}{2}$.

7. a. Use your ruler to draw a line segment $2\frac{1}{4}$ inches long.

b. If you erased $\frac{3}{4}$ inch from this line segment,
how long would the new line segment be? **$1\frac{1}{2}$** in.

8. If you drew a line segment twice as long as the original $2\frac{1}{4}$-inch line
segment, how long would the new line segment be? (Circle one.)

$4\frac{6}{16}$ in. $4\frac{3}{8}$ in.   ($4\frac{2}{4}$ in.) $4\frac{3}{16}$ in.

Add or subtract. Write your answer in simplest form.

9. $\frac{5}{8} + \frac{3}{4} = 1\frac{3}{8}$

10. 1
    $-\frac{2}{3}$
    $\frac{1}{3}$

11. $\frac{5}{8}$
    $-\frac{1}{8}$
    $\frac{1}{8}$

12. $\frac{3}{4}$
    $+1\frac{1}{2}$
    $2\frac{1}{4}$

13. $3\frac{3}{7} - 1\frac{6}{7} = 1\frac{4}{7}$

14. $3\frac{1}{3} + 1\frac{7}{8} = 5\frac{5}{24}$

15. $2\frac{1}{5} - 1\frac{4}{5} = \frac{2}{5}$

Name _____ **Date** _____ **Time** _____

Unit 9 Checking Progress

Use the grid at the right for Problems 1–4.

1. a. Plot and label the following points:

    A: (1,1)   B: (2,3)   C: (5,3)   D: (4,1)

  b. Draw line segments to connect the points as follows:

    A to B, B to C, C to D, and D to A.

  c. Describe the figure you have drawn.

    <u>Sample answer:</u>

    <u>A parallelogram with $\overline{BC}$</u>

    <u>parallel to $\overline{AD}$ and $\overline{AB}$</u>

    <u>parallel to $\overline{CD}$</u>

2. Plot points on the grid to make a reflection of the figure. Begin with the reflection of point A at (1, −1).

3. Record the points you used below.

Point	Original Figure	Reflected Figure
A	(1,1)	(1 , −1)
B	(2,3)	(2 , −3)
C	(5,3)	(5 , −3)
D	(4,1)	(4 , −1)

4. Describe a rule for changing the points from the original figure to get the reflected figure.

<u>Sample answer: Change the second number</u>
<u>in each number pair to its opposite.</u>

Use with Lesson 9.11.

400

Name _____ **Date** _____ **Time** _____

Unit 8 Checking Progress (cont.)

Solve each problem.

16. Bobbie measured the growth of her corn plant every week. One Friday, it was $3\frac{7}{8}$ inches tall. The following Friday, it was $6\frac{3}{8}$ inches tall. How much had it grown in one week? **$2\frac{1}{2}$** in.

17. Explain how you found your answer for Problem 16.

<u>Sample answer: I changed $6\frac{3}{8}$ to $5\frac{11}{8}$. Then I subtracted</u>

<u>$5−3 = 2$, and $\frac{11}{8} − \frac{7}{8} = \frac{4}{8} = \frac{1}{2}$.</u>

18. How many minutes are there in $\frac{1}{3}$ of an hour? **20** min

19. Mary Lou baked 36 cupcakes for the bake sale. If 75% of them had chocolate frosting, how many cupcakes had chocolate frosting? **27** cupcakes

Fill in the missing number.

20. $3\frac{5}{8} = 2\frac{\boxed{13}}{8}$

21. $5\frac{2}{6} = \boxed{4}\frac{8}{6}$

22. $3\frac{1}{7} = 2\frac{\boxed{8}}{7}$

23. $6\frac{5}{9} = \boxed{5}\frac{14}{9}$

24. Fill in the oval next to possible common denominators for each fraction pair. (There may be more than one correct answer.)

  a. $\frac{1}{3}$ and $\frac{4}{9}$
  ○ 3
  ○ 6
  ● 9
  ○ 12

  b. $\frac{3}{4}$ and $\frac{5}{6}$
  ○ 4
  ○ 6
  ● 12
  ● 24

  c. $\frac{5}{8}$ and $\frac{2}{3}$
  ○ 3
  ○ 8
  ○ 12
  ● 24

  d. $\frac{3}{12}$ and $\frac{2}{5}$
  ○ 5
  ○ 7
  ● 30
  ● 60

25. List the eight fractions from Problem 24 in order from smallest to largest.

$\frac{3}{12}$ $\frac{1}{3}$ $\frac{2}{5}$ $\frac{4}{9}$ $\frac{5}{8}$ $\frac{2}{3}$ $\frac{3}{4}$ $\frac{5}{6}$

smallest   largest

Multiply. Write your answer in simplest form.

26. $\frac{3}{8} * \frac{4}{5} = \frac{3}{10}$

27. $\frac{2}{3} * \frac{3}{4} = \frac{1}{2}$

28. $1\frac{1}{2} * 2\frac{3}{5} = 3\frac{9}{10}$

29. $3\frac{1}{5} * 4\frac{5}{8} = 14\frac{4}{5}$

Use with Lesson 8.13.

399

Page 401 (left)

Name   Date   Time

Unit 9 Checking Progress (cont.)

5. Jim wants to build a fence around his rectangular garden. The garden is 15 feet by 5 feet.

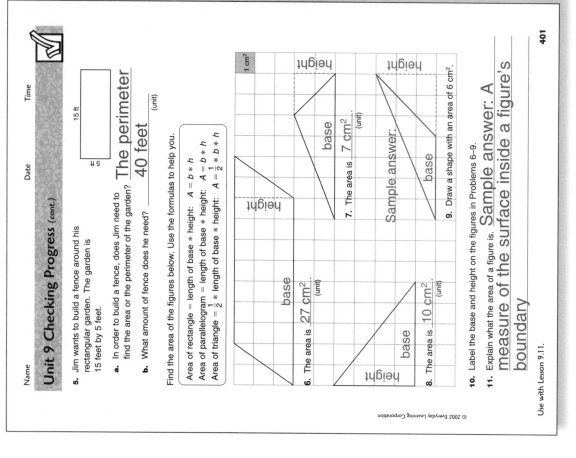

15 ft

5 ft

a. In order to build a fence, does Jim need to find the area or the perimeter of the garden? **The perimeter**

b. What amount of fence does he need? **40 feet**
(unit)

Find the area of the figures below. Use the formulas to help you.

| Area of rectangle = length of base * height: $A = b * h$ |
| Area of parallelogram = length of base * height: $A = b * h$ |
| Area of triangle = $\frac{1}{2}$ * length of base * height: $A = \frac{1}{2} * b * h$ |

1 cm²

height

base

6. The area is **27 cm²**.
(unit)

height

base

7. The area is **7 cm²**.
(unit)

height

base

8. The area is **10 cm²**.
(unit)

base

height

Sample answer:

9. Draw a shape with an area of 6 cm².

10. Label the base and height on the figures in Problems 6–9.

11. Explain what the area of a figure is. **Sample answer: A measure of the surface inside a figure's boundary**

Use with Lesson 9.11.

© 2002 Everyday Learning Corporation

401

Page 402 (right)

© 2002 Everyday Learning Corporation

Name   Date   Time

Unit 9 Checking Progress (cont.)

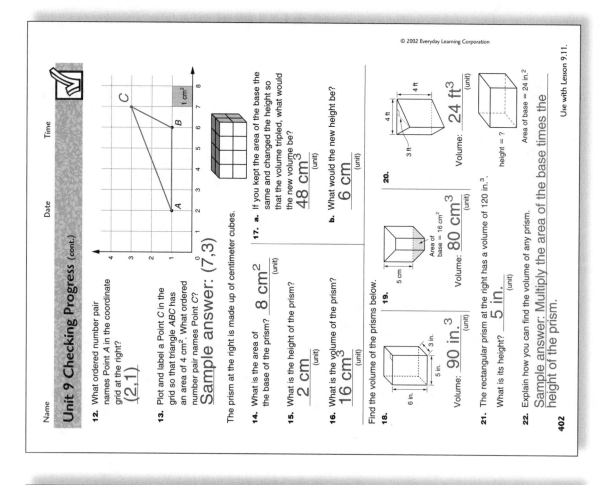

12. What ordered number pair names Point A in the coordinate grid at the right? **(2,1)**

13. Plot and label a Point C in the grid so that triangle ABC has an area of 4 cm². What ordered number pair names Point C? **Sample answer: (7,3)**

1 cm²

The prism at the right is made up of centimeter cubes.

14. What is the area of the base of the prism? **8 cm²**
(unit)

15. What is the height of the prism? **2 cm**
(unit)

16. What is the volume of the prism? **16 cm³**
(unit)

17. a. If you kept the area of the base the same and changed the height, what would the new volume be so that the volume tripled, what would the new volume be? **48 cm³**
(unit)

b. What would the new height be? **6 cm**
(unit)

Find the volume of the prisms below.

18. Volume: **90 in.³**
(unit)

6 in.   5 in.   3 in.

19. Area of base = 16 cm²

5 cm

Volume: **80 cm³**
(unit)

20.

4 ft   4 ft   3 ft

Volume: **24 ft³**
(unit)

21. The rectangular prism at the right has a volume of 120 in.³. What is its height? **5 in.**
(unit)

Area of base = 24 in.²

height = ?

22. Explain how you can find the volume of any prism. **Sample answer: Multiply the area of the base times the height of the prism.**

Use with Lesson 9.11.

402

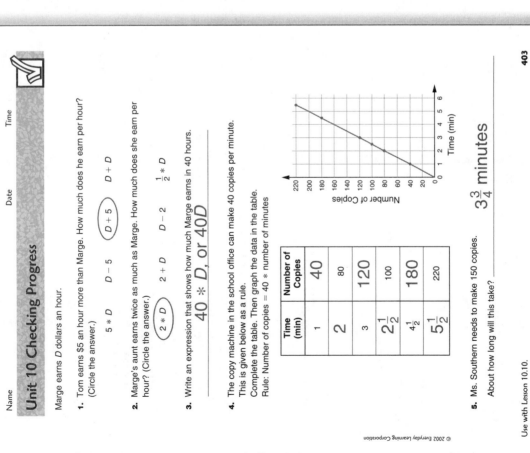

Right page (404)

Unit 10 Checking Progress (cont.)

Solve the pan-balance problems below.

6. One apple weighs
as much as _12_ marbles.

7. One block weighs
as much as _4_ marbles.

8. One ball weighs
as much as _10_ blocks.

9. Shawna wrote an equation but covered one number.
$15 + 7 = \square + 12$. What is the covered number? _10_

10. Pete set up a pan balance. He found that 2 calculators balance 16 marbles.
He then used the pan balance and found that 5 marbles balance 3 marbles
and 10 paper clips. Fill in the blanks below.

a. One calculator weighs as much as _40_ paper clips.

b. One calculator weighs as much as _8_ marbles.

© 2002 Everyday Learning Corporation

Left page (403)

Unit 10 Checking Progress

Marge earns *D* dollars an hour.

1. Tom earns $5 an hour more than Marge. How much does he earn per hour?
(Circle the answer.)

$5 * D$ $D - 5$ $(D + 5)$ $D + D$

2. Marge's aunt earns twice as much as Marge. How much does she earn per
hour? (Circle the answer.)

$(2 * D)$ $2 + D$ $D - 2$ $\frac{1}{2} * D$

3. Write an expression that shows how much Marge earns in 40 hours.

_40 * D, or 40D_

4. The copy machine in the school office can make 40 copies per minute.
This is given below as a rule.
Complete the table. Then graph the data in the table.
Rule: Number of copies = 40 * number of minutes

Time (min)	Number of Copies
1	40
2	80
3	120
$2\frac{1}{2}$	100
$4\frac{1}{2}$	180
$5\frac{1}{2}$	220

5. Ms. Southern needs to make 150 copies.
About how long will this take? _$3\frac{3}{4}$ minutes_

© 2002 Everyday Learning Corporation

Name   Date   Time

Unit 10 Checking Progress (cont.)

Complete each of the following sentences, rounding each answer to the nearest centimeter. Use the π key on your calculator or use 3.14 as an approximation for π.

> Circumference of a circle = π * diameter
>
> Area of a circle = π * radius²

11. The diameter is about ___6___ cm.

12. The radius is about ___3___ cm.

13. The circumference is about ___19___ cm.

14. The area is about ___28___ cm².

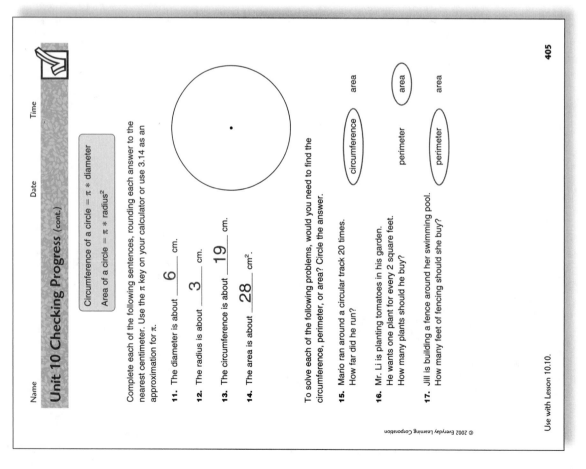

To solve each of the following problems, would you need to find the circumference, perimeter, or area? Circle the answer.

15. Mario ran around a circular track 20 times. How far did he run?

(circumference)   area

16. Mr. Li is planting tomatoes in his garden. He wants one plant for every 2 square feet. How many plants should he buy?

perimeter   (area)

17. Jill is building a fence around her swimming pool. How many feet of fencing should she buy?

(perimeter)   area

Use with Lesson 10.10.

405

Name   Date   Time

Unit 10 Checking Progress (cont.)

18. Mrs. Griffin surveyed her class. She asked three questions. The class made the line plots below to show the results for each question.

Write the number of the line plot next to the question it represents.

- How many complete months are there until your next birthday?   Plot __#1__

- How many years old is the oldest child living at your house?   Plot __#3__

- How many books did you read last summer?   Plot __#2__

Plot #1

```
            X               X   X   X
X   X       X       X   X   X   X   X   X
X   X   X   X   X   X   X   X   X   X   X   X
0   1   2   3   4   5   6   7   8   9   10  11
```

Plot #2

```
    X
    X                       X
X   X                   X   X
X   X   X               X   X
X   X   X   X               X
0   1   2   3   4   5   6   7   8   9   10  11  12  13  14  15  16  17  18  19  20
```

Plot #3

```
X
X
X
X
X               X
X       X   X   X
X   X   X   X   X           X
10  11  12  13  14  15  16  17  18  19  20
```

Use with Lesson 10.10

406

Name   Date   Time

Unit 11 Checking Progress (cont.)

© 2002 Everyday Learning Corporation

Area of rectangle: $A = l * w$	**Circumference of circle:** $C = \pi * d$
Volume of rectangular prism:	**Area of circle:** $A = \pi * r^2$
$V = l * w * h$	**Volume of cylinder:** $V = \pi * r^2 * h$

12. What is the area of the base of the cylinder at the right?

    About 12.6 in.^{2}

    ⌐ 5 in.
    2 in.

13. What is the volume of the cylinder?

    62.8 in.^{3} or 63 in.^{3}

14. What information do you need to know to figure out how many square inches of paint you would use if you painted the entire cylinder (top, bottom, and sides)?

    Sample answer: The height and the radius (or diameter)

15. If you place a cone inside of the cylinder in Problem 13 and the cone is an exact "fit" (that is, the apex of the cone touches the bottom of the cylinder, and the base of the cone fits exactly at the top of the cylinder), what would the volume of the cone be?

    21 in.^{3}

    Write a number sentence to show how you found your answer. $63 \div 3 = 21$

16. Which of the boxes below has the greatest volume?   Box B

    2.5 ft   1.5 ft   2 ft   2 ft   3 ft   1 ft
    2 ft   2 ft   2 ft
    Box A   **Box B**   **Box C**

    Explain how you know. Sample answer: I used the formula $V = l * w * h$ to find the volume of each box. The volume of Box A is 7.5 ft^3, the volume of Box B is 8 ft^3, and the volume of Box C is 6 ft^3.

Name   Date   Time

Unit 11 Checking Progress

Complete each sentence with one of the following names of geometric solids:

    pyramid   cone   rectangular prism   cylinder

1. I have exactly two bases and no vertices. I am a   cylinder .

2. All of my faces are triangular. I am a   pyramid .

3. I have one base and one curved surface. I am a   cone .

4. I have a pair of bases and exactly eight vertices. I am a   rectangular prism .

The prism at the right is made of centimeter cubes.

5. What is the area of the base of the prism?   8 cm^2

6. What is the height of the prism?   2 cm

7. What is the volume of the prism?   16 cm^3

8. What is the surface area of the prism?   40 cm^2

9. Explain how you found your answer for Problem 8.
   Sample answer: The top and bottom areas are each 8 cm^2. The front and back areas are each 8 cm^2. The side areas are each 4 cm^2. $8 + 8 + 8 + 8 + 4 + 4 = 40$ cm^2

10. If you kept the base the same, but tripled the volume of this prism, what would be the height?   6 cm

11. Write a number sentence to show how you solved Problem 10. $48 = 8 * h$

© 2002 Everyday Learning Corporation

Unit 11 Checking Progress (cont.)

Name   Date   Time

17. The rectangular prism at the right has a volume of 120 cubic inches.

What is its height? **5 in.**

height = ?

Area of base = 24 in.²

18. The pyramid at the right has the same height as the prism in Problem 17.

What is the volume of the pyramid? **40 in.³**

Area of base = 24 in.²

Write a number sentence to show how you found your answer. **120 ÷ 3 = 40 or $\frac{1}{3}$ * 24 * 5 = 40**

Joan wants to add medicine to her fish tank. The instructions suggest adding one drop of medicine for every 4 liters of water. The base of Joan's fish tank measures 40 cm by 25 cm. The tank is filled with water to a height of about 20 centimeters.

Reminder: 1 liter = 1,000 cm³

20 cm
25 cm
40 cm

19. How many drops of medicine should Joan add to her tank? **5 drops**

20. Explain what you did to find the answer.

Sample answer: The volume of the water is 20,000 cm³ (40 * 25 * 20), or 20 liters. 20 liters = 5 * 4 liters, so Joan should add 5 drops.

Unit 12 Checking Progress

Name   Date   Time

For each number below, draw a factor tree and write the prime factorization.

Answers vary.

1.

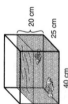

60 = **2 * 2 * 3 * 5**

2.

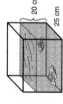

84 = **2 * 2 * 3 * 7**

3. What prime factors do 60 and 84 have in common? **2 and 2 and 3**

4. What is the greatest common factor of 60 and 84? **12**

Explain how you found it. **Sample answer: I multiplied the common prime factors: 2 * 2 * 3 = 12.**

5. What is the least common multiple of 60 and 84? **420**

Explain how you found it. **Sample answer:**

2 * 2 * 3 * 5
2 * 2 * 3 * 7
2 * 2 * 3 * 5 * 7 = 420

Rewrite each fraction pair with a common denominator.

6. $\frac{3}{8}$ and $\frac{5}{12}$ $\frac{9}{24}$ and $\frac{10}{24}$

7. $\frac{6}{7}$ and $\frac{5}{10}$ $\frac{60}{70}$ and $\frac{35}{70}$

8. Explain how you found the answer to Problem 6.

Sample answer: I found the least common multiple of 8 and 12, which is 24. Then I multiplied $\frac{3*3}{8*3}$ and $\frac{5*2}{12*2}$ to get denominators equal to 24.

© 2002 Everyday Learning Corporation

Page 411

Name _____ Date _____ Time _____

Unit 12 Checking Progress (cont.)

9. Darin rolls a 6-sided die and then flips a coin.

How many different ways can the die roll and coin toss turn out? __**12**__ different ways

a. Use the Multiplication Counting Principle to answer.

b. Draw a tree diagram to show all the possible ways.
Suggestion: Use the letters H and T to represent heads and tails.

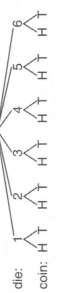

die: 1   2   3   4   5   6

coin: H T H T H T H T H T H T

c. Which method do you think is easier for finding the number of possible results? **Answers vary.**

d. Explain your answer to Part c. **Answers vary.**

10. In Problem 9, what is the probability that Darin

a. rolls a 5 and the coin lands on HEADS? $\frac{1}{12}$

b. rolls an even number and the coin lands on TAILS? $\frac{3}{12}$, or $\frac{1}{4}$

c. rolls a prime number? $\frac{6}{12}$, or $\frac{3}{6}$, or $\frac{1}{2}$

d. tosses the coin so that it lands on HEADS? $\frac{6}{12}$, or $\frac{1}{2}$

Page 412

Name _____ Date _____ Time _____

Unit 12 Checking Progress (cont.)

11. Sven bought a large pizza. He wants to cut the pizza so that it can be shared equally by 2 people, 3 people, 4 people, 6 people, or 8 people. Into how many slices should Sven cut the pizza?

__**24 slices**__
(unit)

12. There are 30 students in Linda's class. Two-thirds of her class rides to school on the school bus. The other students walk to school. How many students walk to school?

__**10 students**__
(unit)

13. Matt was playing *Name That Number.* Of the 5 cards he turned over, 60% were black. How many black cards were there?

__**3 cards**__
(unit)

14. Three out of 7 cars parked on one street were red. If there were 28 cars, how many cars were red?

__**12 cars**__
(unit)

15. What is the ratio of cars that were not red to total cars in Problem 14? $\frac{16}{28}$, or $\frac{4}{7}$

Explain how you found your answer. **Sample answer: Since 12 out of 28 cars were red, 28 − 12 = 16 cars were not red.**

Name Date Time

Unit 12 Checking Progress (cont.)

Write a number model for each problem. Then solve the problem.

16. Rosalyn's family was driving from home to their aunt's house. After going 48 miles, they were $\frac{3}{4}$ of the way there. How far from home was their aunt's house?

Number model: $\dfrac{3}{4} = \dfrac{48}{\square}$

Answer: ___64___ miles

17. In Doreen's first basketball game, she made a basket 9 times out of 15 attempts. She made the same ratio of baskets out of 25 attempts in the second game. How many baskets did she make in her 25 attempts?

Number model: $\dfrac{9}{15} = \dfrac{\square}{25}$

Answer: ___15___ baskets

18. Explain how you found your answer to Problem 17.
Sample answer: $\frac{9}{15} = \frac{3}{5}$. So, the number model can be written as $\frac{3}{5} = \frac{\square}{25} \rightarrow \frac{3*5}{5*5} = \frac{15}{25}$. 9 out of 15 is the same ratio as 15 out of 25. She made 15 baskets.

19. Marcus's heart beats 11 times in 10 seconds. At this rate, about how many times would it beat in 1 minute?

___66___ times

20. Carlo exchanged U.S. dollars for French francs. He got 7 francs for each dollar. He received a total of 224 francs. How many U.S. dollars did he exchange?

___32___ dollars

Use with Lesson 12.10.

Name Date Time

Mid-Year Assessment

Solve the problems below.

1. $28 * 9 =$ ___252___

2. $47 * 68 =$ ___3,196___

3. $235 * 56 =$ ___13,160___

4. $715 + 308 =$ ___1,023___

5. $9.43 + 7.6 =$ ___17.03___

6. $51.2 + 17.6 =$ ___68.8___

7. $247 - 196 =$ ___51___

8. $50.3 - 27.6 =$ ___22.7___

9. $80.3 - 5.17 =$ ___75.13___

Solve for y.

10. $15 - y = 9$ $y = 6$

11. $8 * y = 72$ $y = 9$

12. $150 / y = 30$ $y = 5$

13. Circle all the numbers below that are factors of 48.

②④5⑥⑫1420㉔

Evelyn timed how long it took her to travel to work on nine different days. Following are the times in minutes:

454245554850355844

14. What was the median time? ___45___ minutes

15. What was the maximum time? ___58___ minutes

16. What was the minimum time? ___35___ minutes

17. What was the range of times? ___23___ minutes

18. If you were Evelyn, how much time would you allow to travel to work based on these data? ___About 1 hour___

19. Explain your answer to Problem 18.
Sample answer: I would allow at least the maximum (58 minutes) so that I was sure to be on time.

Use with Lesson 6.11.

Name   Date   Time

Mid-Year Assessment (cont.)

20. Circle all of the numbers below that are greater than $\frac{1}{2}$.

$\frac{1}{4}$ (**$\frac{9}{10}$**)   (**0.66**) $\frac{5}{20}$ $\frac{4}{8}$ 0.09

21. On the back of this page, draw a rectangle that has a base 4 cm long and a height of 6.5 cm. Use your ruler or any other tool that you wish.

22. Find the perimeter of the rectangle you drew on the back of this page.

Perimeter: __21 cm__
           (unit)

23. Circle all of the expressions below that are equivalent to $\frac{3}{4}$.

(**0.75**) $\frac{8}{6}$ $\frac{6}{12}$ $\frac{9}{16}$ (**$\frac{15}{20}$**)   34%

24. Measure each angle below. Record your answer to the nearest degree.

∠TOP measures about __25__°.

∠BAG measures about __110__°.

25. Circle the obtuse angle in Problem 24.

26. Plot the following points on the grid to the right. Connect the points.

(2,1), (3,3), (6,3), (5,1)

27. What shape did you draw in Problem 26? __parallelogram__

28. Give two other names for the shape you drew in Problem 26.

__quadrangle__   __polygon__

Name   Date   Time

Mid-Year Assessment (cont.)

29. Jianhua buys a carton of milk for 59 cents, a hamburger for $1.25, and a salad for $1.50. He pays with a five-dollar bill.

How much did he spend? __$3.34__

How much change should he get? __$1.66__

30. Name a number between 400 and 500 that is divisible by 3 but not by 2.   __441__   Sample answer:

Explain how you found your number.

Sample answer: I know that $4 + 1 + 4$ is equal to a multiple of 3 (9). Any number whose digits add up to a multiple of 3 is divisible by 3. I rearranged those three digits to get 441. Since it is not even, it is not divisible by 2.

31. Is 71 prime or composite? __prime__

Explain how you know.

Sample answer: It is prime because it has only itself and 1 as factors.

32. Round to the nearest...

thousand.

65,389	65,000
104,032	104,000
1,029,754	1,030,000

33. tenth.

0.784	0.8
17.493	17.5
25.815	25.8

Name   Date   Time

Mid-Year Assessment (cont.)

34. Explain the errors in the following problem.

```
   24
 * 96
   18
  360
   12
  240
  630
```

Sample answer: The person multiplied 9 * 2 and 6 * 2 instead of 90 * 20 and 6 * 20. Also, this person did 6 * 40 instead of 6 * 4.

35. Make a magnitude estimate for the product in Problem 34. Circle the appropriate box.

10s   100s   (1000s)   10,000s

36. Write the 8-digit number that has a 4 in the hundreds place, a 5 in the thousandths place, a 9 in the ten-thousandths place and 1s in all other places.

9 1 , 4 1 1 . 1 1 5

Write this number in words:

ninety-one thousand, four hundred eleven and one hundred fifteen thousandths

Add. Use the fraction sticks to help.

37. $\frac{1}{2} + \frac{1}{4} = $ $\frac{3}{4}$

38. $\frac{3}{8} + \frac{1}{4} = $ $\frac{5}{8}$

39. $\frac{3}{4} + \frac{3}{4} = $ $\frac{6}{4}$, or $1\frac{1}{2}$

40. $\frac{1}{8} + \frac{1}{2} = $ $\frac{5}{8}$

417

Name   Date   Time

Mid-Year Assessment (cont.)

Simeon was writing a report on trees in his town. He counted the different types of trees in his neighborhood and made a circle graph. Use his circle graph to answer these questions:

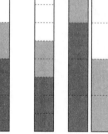

Maples 42%   Elms 28%   Pines and other evergreens 16%   Oaks 10%   Other

41. What was the most common type of tree? __maple__

42. Which types of trees made up one-fourth or more of the sample?
Maples and elms

43. If there were a total of 200 trees in his sample, how many would be oaks? __20 oaks__

Explain how you got your answer.
Sample answer: I know that for every one hundred trees, about ten of them are oaks, so if there were twice as many trees, there would be twice as many, or 20, oak trees.

44. Simeon concluded that maples are the most common type of tree in the U.S. Do you agree? __No__
Explain. Sample answer: No, because this is only a survey of Simeon's town.

418

Name   Date   Time

End-of-Year Assessment

1. A figure is partly hidden. Which of the following might it be? (Circle all possible answers.)

(rectangle)   triangle   (trapezoid)   square

2. A package of hot-dog buns contains 12 buns. Mrs. Hudson is expecting 35 people at her picnic. She wants to have enough hot dog buns for each person to have 2. How many packages of buns should she buy? __6 packages__

3. Below is a data set. Put two more numbers in it so that

- the median of the new data set is 5,
- the maximum is 15, and
- the range is 13.

4   5   4   11   8   __2__   __15__

4. A board is $6\frac{1}{8}$ inches long. If you cut off $\frac{3}{4}$ of an inch, how much is left? __$\frac{43}{8}$, or $5\frac{3}{8}$__ inches

5. Jean combined $\frac{1}{3}$ cup of corn flour with $\frac{3}{4}$ cup of white flour. Is the total flour more or less than 1 cup? __more__
Explain. __Sample answer: It has to be more than a cup because $\frac{1}{3}$ is larger than $\frac{1}{4}$ and $\frac{3}{4} + \frac{1}{4}$ is one cup.__

Use with Lesson 12.10.

419

Name   Date   Time

End-of-Year Assessment (cont.)

For each fraction below, circle all the numbers to the right of the fraction that are equivalent to it.

6. $\frac{3}{8}$ $\frac{6}{16}$ 1.25   38% $\frac{24}{64}$ 0.375

7. $\frac{6}{10}$ 0.600 $\frac{3}{5}$ $\frac{2}{3}$ 60%   0.6

8. $\frac{19}{20}$ 0.95   19% $\frac{38}{40}$ $\frac{48}{50}$ 95%

Each square in the grid below has an area of 1 square centimeter.

9. What is the area of triangle END? __10__ cm²

10. Draw a rectangle that has an area of 12 cm². See sample answer below.

11. What is the perimeter of this rectangle? __16__ cm (Sample answer)

Sample answer:

12. What is the volume of the prism to the right? __24 in.³__ (unit)

Volume of a prism: $V = B * h$

13. A cylindrical can has a base with an area of 21.5 square centimeters. It has a height of 10 centimeters. What is its volume? __215 cm³__ (unit)

Volume of a cylinder: $V = B * h$

14. Write the 8-digit number that has a 5 in the tens place, a 3 in the hundredths place, a 4 in the hundred-thousands place, and 8 in all the other places. __4 8 8, 8 5 8 . 8 3__

15. Write the number that is 4,000 less than the number you wrote in Problem 14. __484,858.83__

420

Use with Lesson 12.10.

End-of-Year Assessment (cont.)

Name   Date   Time

28. In the space below, draw a circle that has a radius of 3 cm.

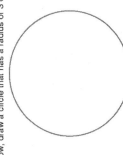

29. Calculate the circumference and area of the circle you drew in Problem 28.

> Circumference of a circle: $C = \pi * d$
> Area of a circle: $A = \pi * r^2$

Circumference = $\underline{18.8\ cm}$ Area = $\underline{28.3\ cm^2}$
(unit)   (unit)

30. Describe a situation for which you would calculate circumference.

Sample answer: I might want to know circumference if I am going to put a fence around a swimming pool.

Solve. Do not use a calculator.

31. $756 \div 9 = \underline{84}$ **32.** $308 * 42 = \underline{12,936}$ **33.** $312 \div 12 = \underline{26}$

34. $5.63 * 28 = \underline{157.64}$ **35.** $92.4 / 6 = \dfrac{15.4}{11}$ **36.** $4.6 * 24.8 = \underline{114.08}$

37. $3\frac{1}{2} + 2\frac{1}{8} = \dfrac{5\frac{5}{8}}{}$ **38.** $2\frac{1}{8} - \frac{5}{3} = \dfrac{}{24}$ **39.** $3\frac{5}{10} + \frac{3}{4} = \underline{4\frac{1}{4}}$

End-of-Year Assessment (cont.)

Name   Date   Time

16. Round the number you wrote in Problem 15 to the nearest tenth. $\underline{484,858.8}$ thousand. $\underline{485,000}$

17. Mark the following points on the ruler.

A: $\frac{7}{8}$ B: $\frac{3}{4}$ C: $\frac{5}{16}$ D: $2\frac{11}{16}$ E: $\frac{5}{10}$

Use $>$, $<$, or $=$.

18. $\frac{3}{8} \underline{<} \frac{3}{7}$ **19.** $0.38 \underline{>} \frac{3}{10}$ **20.** $3\frac{2}{3} \underline{>} \frac{24}{10}$

21. $0.05 \underline{<} \frac{5}{10}$ **22.** $\frac{18}{25} \underline{=} 72\%$ **23.** $\frac{5}{15} \underline{<} 0.66$

24. What is the probability of drawing a king of hearts from a regular deck of 52 cards? $\dfrac{1}{52}$, or about 2%

25. What is the probability of drawing a 5 from a regular deck of 52 cards? $\dfrac{4}{52}$, or about 8%

26. Measure the angles below.

$\angle JAM$ measures about $\underline{230°}$. $\angle FIN$ measures about $\underline{90°}$

27. Circle the reflex angle in Problem 26.
What is the name of the other angle? $\underline{\text{right angle}}$

Name   Date   Time

End-of-Year Assessment (cont.)

40. Write the prime factorization for 186. $2 * 3 * 31$

41. Mr. Taylor's science class asked 50 students each to name their favorite pet.
The results are shown in the table. Complete the percent column of the table.

Animal	Number	Percent
Cat	21	42%
Dog	13	26%
Hamster or Gerbil	4	8%
Bird	8	16%
Other	4	8%
Total	50	100%

42. Did more than $\frac{1}{2}$ or less than $\frac{1}{2}$ of the
students name cat or dog as their favorite?   More than half

43. What pet was named by about $\frac{1}{4}$ of the students?   dog

44. What percent do you think named snake as their favorite pet? (Circle the best answer.)

4%   (not more than 8%)   at least 4 of the students

Explain. Sample answer: I circled "not more than
8%" because 8% is how many students
chose "other." I know that more than that
could not have chosen snake.

Use with Lesson 12.10.

Name   Date   Time

End-of-Year Assessment (cont.)

45. Draw a circle graph for the information in Problem 41. Label each section.
Use your percent circle on your Geometry Template.

Favorite Pets

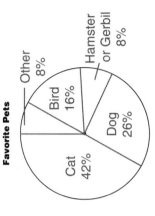

Cat 42%
Dog 26%
Bird 16%
Other 8%
Hamster or Gerbil 8%

Write >, <, or =.

46. -3 __<__ 3

47. -15 __<__ -10

48. $-5 + -3$ __>__ -12

49. $-7 + 7$ __=__ 0

50. $-4 - (-8)$ __>__ $2 + -5$

51. $17 + (-3)$ __<__ $10 + 10$

52. Circle the number sentences that are true.

$$\boxed{5 + (7 * 5) = 40}$$ $$\boxed{36 = 2^2 + 4 * 8}$$ $$30 / (2 + 8) + 5 = 28$$

$$0 = (-5 + 3) * 2$$ $$\boxed{40 - 15 / 5 + 2 = 39}$$ $$18 / 3 + 3 * 4 = \frac{3}{4}$$

Find the greatest common factor for each pair of numbers below.

53. 24 and 60   12

54. 100 and 25   25

Find the least common multiple for each pair of numbers below.

55. 4 and 8   8

56. 6 and 9   18

Use with Lesson 12.10.

End-of-Year Assessment (cont.)

Name   Date   Time

57. Complete the table. Then graph the data in the table.

Rule: Number of words = minutes * 46 words

Time (min)	Number of words
1	46
4	184
3	138
2	92
2.5	115

Number of Words — 20 40 60 80 100 120 140 160 180 200

Time (minutes) — 0 1 2 3 4 5

Write a number model for the problem. Then solve the problem.

58. Maureen was cleaning her collection of elephant toys. She had already cleaned 24 of them. If she had cleaned $\frac{6}{7}$ of them, how many did she have left to clean?

Number model: $24 \div 6 = 4$

Answer: __4 elephants__
        (unit)

Explain. Sample answer: If she had finished $\frac{6}{7}$, I can divide 24 by 6 to find out how many are in one seventh. The answer is 4.

59. Name at least two characteristics that a cone and a cylinder share.

Explain. Sample answer: Both have one curved surface, and both have a circle for a base.

Use with Lesson 12.10.

425

End-of-Year Assessment (cont.)

Name   Date   Time

60. Circle the figure below that has the greatest volume.

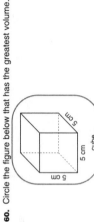

cube — 5 cm, 5 cm, 5 cm

cone — 5 cm, 5 cm

square pyramid — 5 cm, 5 cm, 5 cm

Volume of a prism: $V = B * h$

Volume of a cone: $V = \frac{1}{3} * (B * h)$

Volume of a pyramid: $V = \frac{1}{3} * (B * h)$

Explain. Sample answer: The cube would have the largest volume. The pyramid would be $\frac{1}{3}$ of the volume because it has the same area for the base as the cube, but then you have to divide by 3. The cone would be smaller because the area of its base is smaller than that of the cube, and then you still have to divide it by 3.

Write each fraction in its simplest form.

61. $\frac{28}{3} = 9\frac{1}{3}$

62. $4\frac{18}{24} = 4\frac{3}{4}$

63. $\frac{43}{6} = 7\frac{1}{6}$

64. $\frac{70}{5} = 14$

65. $9\frac{36}{60} = 9\frac{3}{5}$

66. $11\frac{54}{72} = 11\frac{3}{4}$

Use with Lesson 12.10.

426

Class Checklist: Unit 1

Class _____

Dates _____

Use with Lesson 1.10.

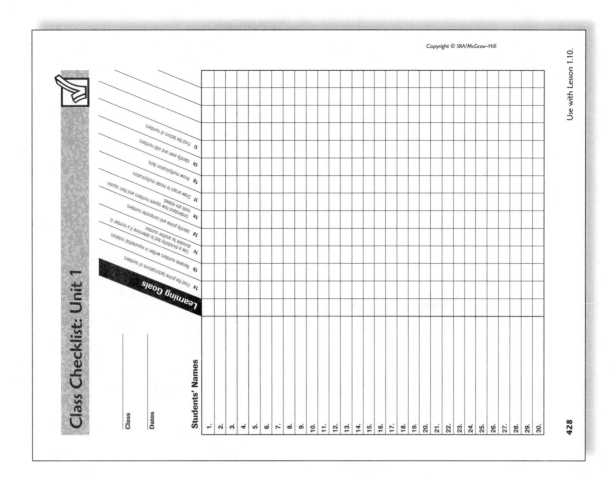

Learning Goals

1a Find the prime factorizations of numbers.

1b Rename numbers written in exponential notation.

1c Use a divisibility test to determine if a number is divisible by another number.

1d Identify prime and composite numbers.

1e Understand how square numbers and their square roots are related.

1f Draw arrays to model multiplication.

1g Know multiplication facts.

1h Identify even and odd numbers.

1i Find the factors of numbers.

Students' Names

1.
2.
3.
4.
5.
6.
7.
8.
9.
10.
11.
12.
13.
14.
15.
16.
17.
18.
19.
20.
21.
22.
23.
24.
25.
26.
27.
28.
29.
30.

428

Class Checklist: Unit 2

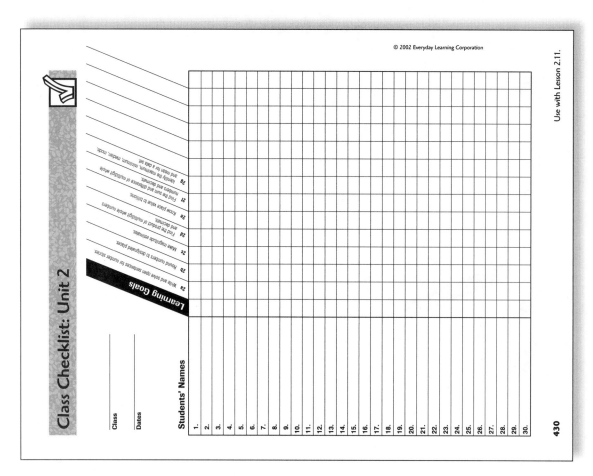

Class _____

Dates _____

Students' Names

Learning Goals

2a	Write and solve open sentences for number stories.							
2b	Round numbers to designated places.							
2c	Make magnitude estimates.							
2d	Find the product of multidigit whole numbers and decimals.							
2e	Know place value to billions.							
2f	Find the sum and difference of multidigit whole numbers and decimals.							
2g	Identify the maximum, minimum, median, mode, and mean for a data set.							

1.
2.
3.
4.
5.
6.
7.
8.
9.
10.
11.
12.
13.
14.
15.
16.
17.
18.
19.
20.
21.
22.
23.
24.
25.
26.
27.
28.
29.
30.

Use with Lesson 2.11.

430

Student's Name _____ Date _____

Individual Profile of Progress: Unit 1

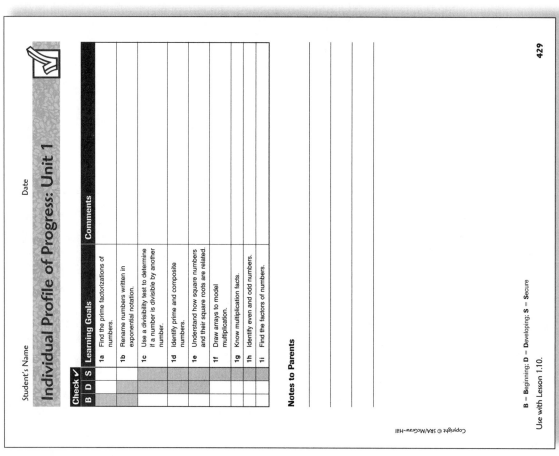

Check ✓			Learning Goals	Comments
B	**D**	**S**		
			1a Find the prime factorizations of numbers.	
			1b Rename numbers written in exponential notation.	
			1c Use a divisibility test to determine if a number is divisible by another number.	
			1d Identify prime and composite numbers.	
			1e Understand how square numbers and their square roots are related.	
			1f Draw arrays to model multiplication.	
			1g Know multiplication facts.	
			1h Identify even and odd numbers.	
			1i Find the factors of numbers.	

Notes to Parents

_____

_____

_____

_____

B = Beginning; **D** = Developing; **S** = Secure

Use with Lesson 1.10.

429

Class Checklist: Unit 3

Class _____

Dates _____

Learning Goals

3a	Determine angle measures based on relationships between angles.
3b	Estimate the measure of an angle.
3c	Measure an angle to within 2°.
3d	Identify types of angles.
3e	Identify types of triangles.
3f	Identify place value in numbers to billions.
3g	Know properties of polygons.
3h	Define and create tessellations.

Students' Names

1.
2.
3.
4.
5.
6.
7.
8.
9.
10.
11.
12.
13.
14.
15.
16.
17.
18.
19.
20.
21.
22.
23.
24.
25.
26.
27.
28.
29.
30.

Use with Lesson 3.11.

432

Student's Name _____ Date _____

Individual Profile of Progress: Unit 2

Check ✓			Learning Goals	Comments
B	**D**	**S**		
			2a Write and solve open sentences for number stories.	
			2b Round numbers to designated places.	
			2c Make magnitude estimates.	
			2d Find the product of multidigit whole numbers and decimals.	
			2e Know place value to billions.	
			2f Find the sum and difference of multidigit whole numbers and decimals.	
			2g Identify the maximum, minimum, median, mode, and mean for a data set.	

Notes to Parents

B = Beginning; **D** = Developing; **S** = Secure

Use with Lesson 2.11.

431

Class Checklist: Unit 4

Class _____

Dates _____

Learning Goals

4a Divide decimal numbers by whole numbers with no remainders.

4b Write and solve number sentences with variables for division number stories.

4c Find the quotient and remainder of a whole number divided by a 1-digit whole number.

4d Find the quotient and remainder of a whole number divided by a 2-digit whole number.

4e Make magnitude estimates for quotients of whole and decimal numbers divided by whole numbers.

4f Interpret the remainder in division number stories.

4g Determine the value of a variable; use this value to complete a number sentence.

4h Know place value to hundredths.

Students' Names

1.
2.
3.
4.
5.
6.
7.
8.
9.
10.
11.
12.
13.
14.
15.
16.
17.
18.
19.
20.
21.
22.
23.
24.
25.
26.
27.
28.
29.
30.

Use with Lesson 4.7.

434

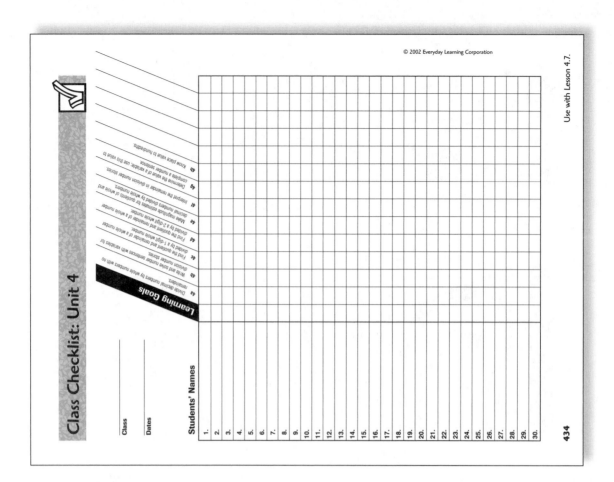

Student's Name _____ Date _____

Individual Profile of Progress: Unit 3

Check ✓			Learning Goals	Comments
B	D	S		
			3a Determine angle measures based on relationships between angles.	
			3b Estimate the measure of an angle.	
			3c Measure an angle to within 2°.	
			3d Identify types of angles.	
			3e Identify types of triangles.	
			3f Identify place value in numbers to billions.	
			3g Know properties of polygons.	
			3h Define and create tessellations.	

Notes to Parents

B = Beginning; D = Developing; S = Secure

Use with Lesson 3.11.

433

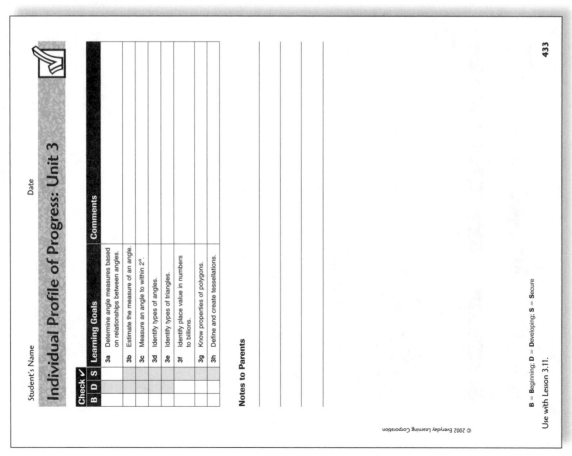

Class Checklist: Unit 5

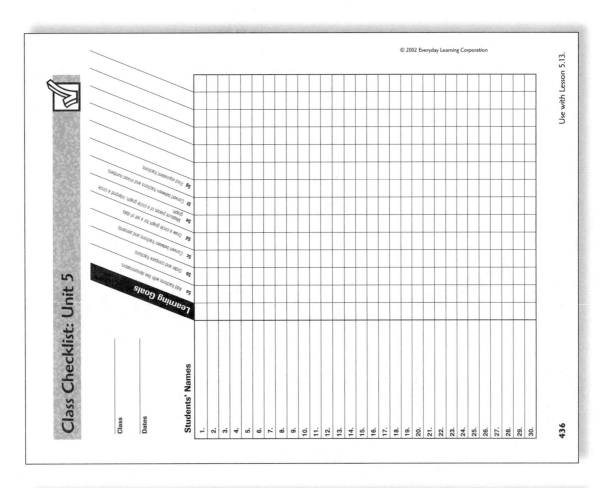

Class _____

Dates _____

Learning Goals

5a Add fractions with like denominators.
5b Order and compare fractions.
5c Convert between fractions and percents.
5d Draw a circle graph for a set of data.
5e Measure pieces of a circle graph. Interpret a circle graph.
5f Convert between fractions and mixed numbers.
5g Find equivalent fractions.

Students' Names

1.
2.
3.
4.
5.
6.
7.
8.
9.
10.
11.
12.
13.
14.
15.
16.
17.
18.
19.
20.
21.
22.
23.
24.
25.
26.
27.
28.
29.
30.

Use with Lesson 5.13.

436

Student's Name _____ Date _____

Individual Profile of Progress: Unit 4

Check ✓			Learning Goals	Comments
B	**D**	**S**		
			4a Divide decimal numbers by whole numbers with no remainders.	
			4b Write and solve number sentences with variables for division number stories.	
			4c Find the quotient and remainder of a whole number divided by a 1-digit whole number.	
			4d Find the quotient and remainder of a whole number divided by a 2-digit whole number.	
			4e Make magnitude estimates for quotients of whole and decimal numbers divided by whole numbers.	
			4f Interpret the remainder in division number stories.	
			4g Determine the value of a variable; use this value to complete a number sentence.	
			4h Know place value to hundredths.	

Notes to Parents

B = Beginning; **D** = Developing; **S** = Secure

Use with Lesson 4.7.

435

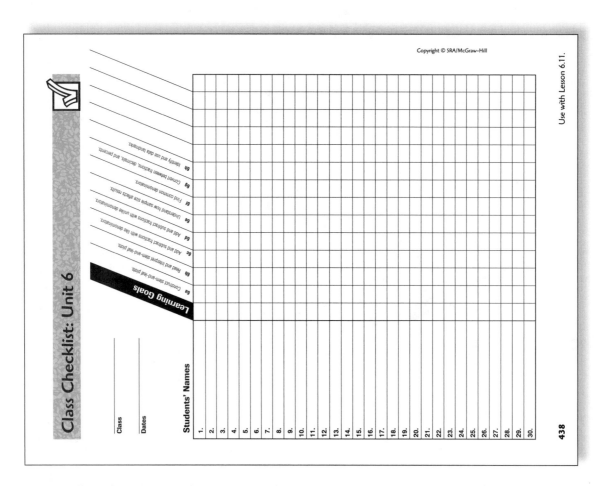

Class Checklist: Unit 6

Class _____

Dates _____

Learning Goals

- 5a Construct stem-and-leaf plots
- 5b Read and interpret stem-and-leaf plots
- 5c Add and subtract fractions with like denominators.
- 5d Add and subtract fractions with unlike denominators.
- 5e Understand how sample size affects results
- 5f Find common denominators.
- 5g Convert between fractions, decimals, and percents.
- 5h Identify and use data landmarks.

Students' Names

1.
2.
3.
4.
5.
6.
7.
8.
9.
10.
11.
12.
13.
14.
15.
16.
17.
18.
19.
20.
21.
22.
23.
24.
25.
26.
27.
28.
29.
30.

Use with Lesson 6.11.

438

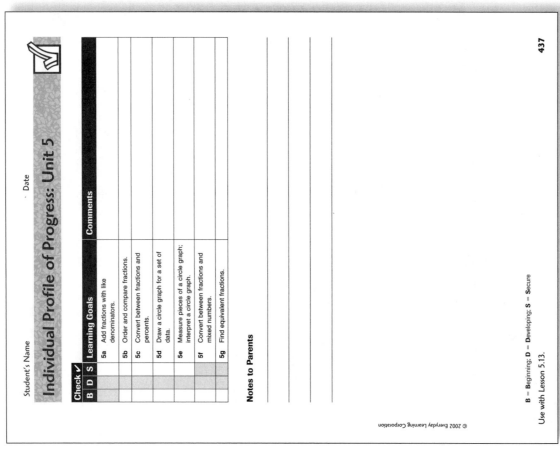

Student's Name _____ · Date _____

Individual Profile of Progress: Unit 5

Check ✔			Learning Goals	Comments
B	**D**	**S**		
			5a Add fractions with like denominators.	
			5b Order and compare fractions.	
			5c Convert between fractions and percents.	
			5d Draw a circle graph for a set of data.	
			5e Measure pieces of a circle graph; interpret a circle graph.	
			5f Convert between fractions and mixed numbers.	
			5g Find equivalent fractions.	

Notes to Parents

B = Beginning; **D** = Developing; **S** = Secure

Use with Lesson 5.13.

437

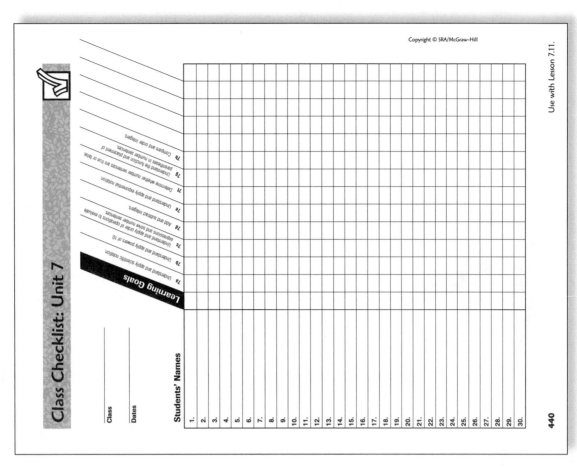

Class Checklist: Unit 7

Class _____

Dates _____

Learning Goals

- 7a Understand and apply scientific notation.
- 7b Understand and apply powers of 10.
- 7c Understand and apply order of operations to evaluate expressions and solve number sentences.
- 7d Add and subtract integers.
- 7e Understand and apply exponential notation.
- 7f Determine whether number sentences are true or false.
- 7g Understand the function and placement of parentheses in number sentences.
- 7h Compare and order integers.

Students' Names

1.
2.
3.
4.
5.
6.
7.
8.
9.
10.
11.
12.
13.
14.
15.
16.
17.
18.
19.
20.
21.
22.
23.
24.
25.
26.
27.
28.
29.
30.

Use with Lesson 7.11.

440

Student's Name _____   Date _____

Individual Profile of Progress: Unit 6

Check ✓			Learning Goals	Comments
B	**D**	**S**		
			6a Construct stem-and-leaf plots.	
			6b Read and interpret stem-and-leaf plots.	
			6c Add and subtract fractions with like denominators.	
			6d Add and subtract fractions with unlike denominators.	
			6e Understand how sample size affects results.	
			6f Find common denominators.	
			6g Convert between fractions, decimals, and percents.	
			6h Identify and use data landmarks.	

Notes to Parents

_____

_____

_____

_____

B = Beginning; **D** = Developing; **S** = Secure

Use with Lesson 6.11.

439

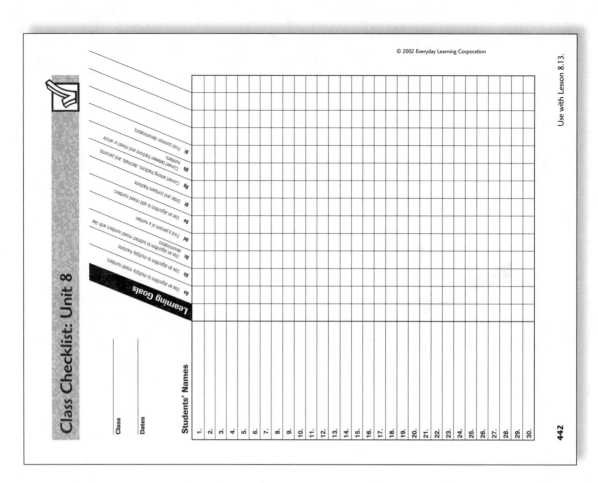

Class Checklist: Unit 8

Class _____

Dates _____

Learning Goals

- **8a** Use an algorithm to multiply mixed numbers.
- **8b** Use an algorithm to multiply fractions.
- **8c** Use an algorithm to subtract mixed numbers with like denominators.
- **8d** Find a percent of a number.
- **8e** Use an algorithm to add mixed numbers.
- **8f** Order and compare fractions.
- **8g** Convert among fractions, decimals, and percents.
- **8h** Convert between fractions and mixed or whole numbers.
- **8i** Find common denominators.

Students' Names

1. 2. 3. 4. 5. 6. 7. 8. 9. 10. 11. 12. 13. 14. 15. 16. 17. 18. 19. 20. 21. 22. 23. 24. 25. 26. 27. 28. 29. 30.

© 2002 Everyday Learning Corporation

Use with Lesson 8.13.

442

Student's Name _____   Date _____

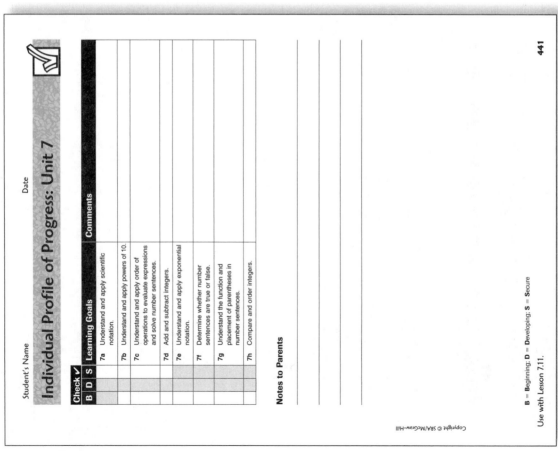

Individual Profile of Progress: Unit 7

Check ✔			Learning Goals	Comments
B	**D**	**S**		
			7a Understand and apply scientific notation.	
			7b Understand and apply powers of 10.	
			7c Understand and apply order of operations to evaluate expressions and solve number sentences.	
			7d Add and subtract integers.	
			7e Understand and apply exponential notation.	
			7f Determine whether number sentences are true or false.	
			7g Understand the function and placement of parentheses in number sentences.	
			7h Compare and order integers.	

Notes to Parents

_____

_____

_____

B = Beginning; **D** = Developing; **S** = Secure

Use with Lesson 7.11.

Copyright © SRA/McGraw-Hill

441

Class Checklist: Unit 9

Class _____

Dates _____

Learning Goals

9a Plot ordered pairs on a four-quadrant coordinate grid.

9b Understand the concept of volume of a figure.

9c Use a formula to find the volume of prisms.

9d Plot ordered pairs on a one-quadrant coordinate grid.

9e Identify the base and height of triangles and parallelograms.

9f Use a formula to find the area of triangles and parallelograms.

9g Understand the concept of area of a figure.

9h Use a formula to find the area of rectangles.

Students' Names

1.
2.
3.
4.
5.
6.
7.
8.
9.
10.
11.
12.
13.
14.
15.
16.
17.
18.
19.
20.
21.
22.
23.
24.
25.
26.
27.
28.
29.
30.

Use with Lesson 9.11.

444

Student's Name _____ Date _____

Individual Profile of Progress: Unit 8

Check ✓			Learning Goals	Comments
B	D	S		
			8a Use an algorithm to multiply mixed numbers.	
			8b Use an algorithm to multiply fractions.	
			8c Use an algorithm to subtract mixed numbers with like denominators.	
			8d Find a percent of a number.	
			8e Use an algorithm to add mixed numbers.	
			8f Order and compare fractions.	
			8g Convert among fractions, decimals, and percents.	
			8h Convert between fractions and mixed or whole numbers.	
			8i Find common denominators.	

Notes to Parents

_____

_____

_____

_____

B = Beginning; **D** = Developing; **S** = Secure

Use with Lesson 8.13.

443

Class Checklist: Unit 10

Class _____

Dates _____

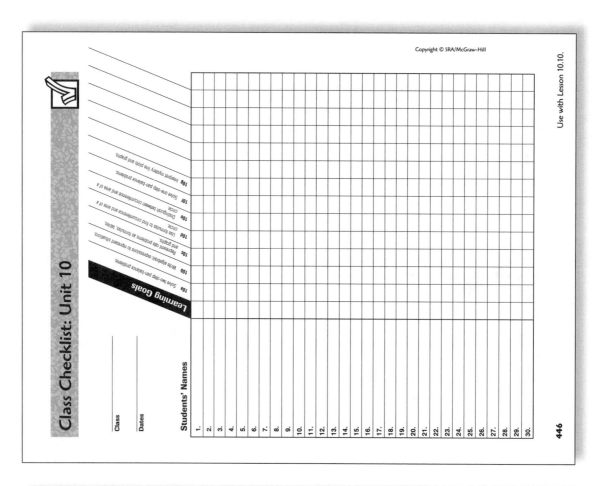

Learning Goals

10a Solve two-step pan-balance problems.

10b Write algebraic expressions to represent situations.

10c Represent rate problems as formulas, tables, and graphs.

10d Use formulas to find circumference and area of a circle.

10e Use formulas to find circumference and area of a circle.

10f Distinguish between circumference and area of a circle.

10g Solve one-step pan-balance problems.

10h Interpret mystery line plots and graphs.

Students' Names

1.
2.
3.
4.
5.
6.
7.
8.
9.
10.
11.
12.
13.
14.
15.
16.
17.
18.
19.
20.
21.
22.
23.
24.
25.
26.
27.
28.
29.
30.

Use with Lesson 10.10.

446

Student's Name _____   Date _____

Individual Profile of Progress: Unit 9

Check ✔			Learning Goals	Comments
B	D	S		
			9a Plot ordered pairs on a four-quadrant coordinate grid.	
			9b Understand the concept of volume of a figure.	
			9c Use a formula to find the volume of prisms.	
			9d Plot ordered pairs on a one-quadrant coordinate grid.	
			9e Identify the base and height of triangles and parallelograms.	
			9f Use a formula to find the area of triangles and parallelograms.	
			9g Understand the concept of area of a figure.	
			9h Use a formula to find the area of rectangles.	

Notes to Parents

_____

_____

_____

_____

B = Beginning; **D** = Developing; **S** = Secure

Use with Lesson 9.11.

445

Class Checklist: Unit 11

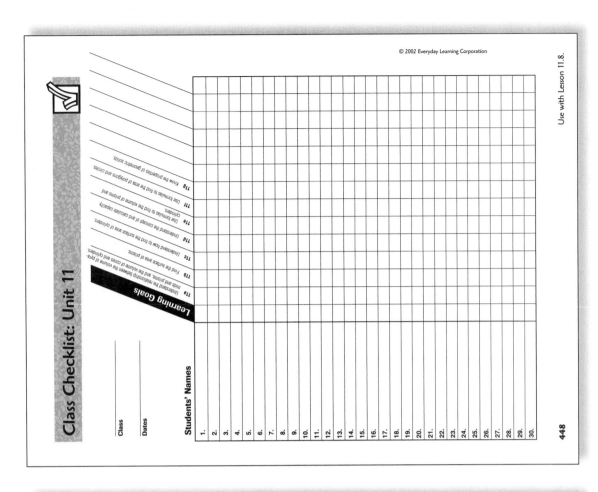

Class _____

Dates _____

Learning Goals

11a Understand the relationship between the volume of pyramids and prisms, and the volume of cones and cylinders.

11b Find the surface area of prisms.

11c Understand how to find the surface area of cylinders.

11d Understand the concept of and calculate capacity.

11e Use formulas to find the volume of prisms and cylinders.

11f Use formulas to find the area of polygons and circles.

11g Know the properties of geometric solids.

Students' Names

1.
2.
3.
4.
5.
6.
7.
8.
9.
10.
11.
12.
13.
14.
15.
16.
17.
18.
19.
20.
21.
22.
23.
24.
25.
26.
27.
28.
29.
30.

Use with Lesson 11.8.

448

Student's Name _____   Date _____

Individual Profile of Progress: Unit 10

Check ✔			Learning Goals	Comments
B	D	S		
			10a Solve two-step pan-balance problems.	
			10b Write algebraic expressions to represent situations.	
			10c Represent rate problems as formulas, tables, and graphs.	
			10d Use formulas to find circumference and area of a circle.	
			10e Distinguish between circumference and area of a circle.	
			10f Solve one-step pan-balance problems.	
			10g Interpret mystery line plots and graphs.	

Notes to Parents

_____

_____

_____

B = Beginning; **D** = Developing; **S** = Secure

Use with Lesson 10.10.

447

Class Checklist: Unit 12

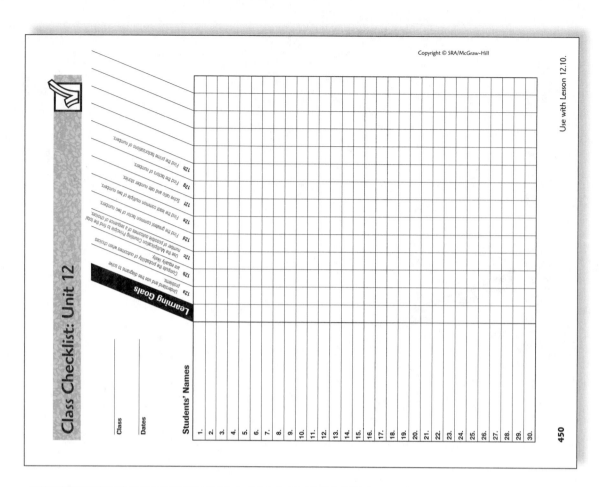

Copyright © SRA/McGraw-Hill

Class _____

Dates _____

Learning Goals

12a Understand and use the diagrams to solve problems.
12b Compute the probability of outcomes when choices are equally likely.
12c Use the Multiplication Counting Principle to find the total number of possible outcomes of a sequence of choices.
12d Find the greatest common factor of two numbers.
12e Find the least common multiple of two numbers.
12f Solve ratio and rate number stories.
12g Find the factors of numbers.
12h Find the prime factorizations of numbers.

Students' Names

1.
2.
3.
4.
5.
6.
7.
8.
9.
10.
11.
12.
13.
14.
15.
16.
17.
18.
19.
20.
21.
22.
23.
24.
25.
26.
27.
28.
29.
30.

450

Use with Lesson 12.10.

Student's Name _____ Date _____

Individual Profile of Progress: Unit 11

Check ✔			Learning Goals	Comments
B	**D**	**S**		
			11a Understand the relationship between the volume of pyramids and prisms, and the volume of cones and cylinders.	
			11b Find the surface area of prisms.	
			11c Understand how to find the surface area of cylinders.	
			11d Understand the concept of and calculate capacity.	
			11e Use formulas to find the volume of prisms and cylinders.	
			11f Use formulas to find the area of polygons and circles.	
			11g Know the properties of geometric solids.	

Notes to Parents

B = Beginning; D = Developing; S = Secure

Use with Lesson 11.8.

449

Class Checklist: 1st Quarter

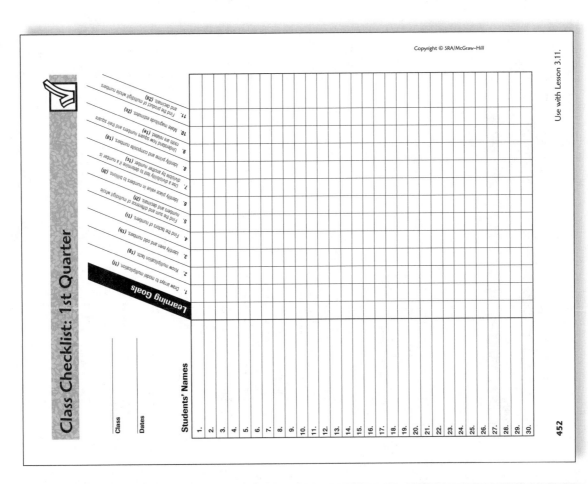

Class _____

Dates _____

Learning Goals

1. Draw arrays to model multiplication. (1f)
2. Know multiplication facts. (1g)
3. Identify even and odd numbers. (1h)
4. Find the factors of numbers. (1i)
5. Find the sum and difference of multidigit whole numbers and decimals. (2j)
6. Identify place value in numbers to billions. (3f)
7. Use a divisibility test to determine if a number is divisible by another number. (1c)
8. Identify prime and composite numbers. (1d)
9. Understand how square numbers and their square roots are related. (1e)
10. Make magnitude estimates. (2c)
11. Find the product of multidigit whole numbers and decimals. (2d)

Students' Names

1.
2.
3.
4.
5.
6.
7.
8.
9.
10.
11.
12.
13.
14.
15.
16.
17.
18.
19.
20.
21.
22.
23.
24.
25.
26.
27.
28.
29.
30.

452

Use with Lesson 3.11.

Student's Name _____   Date _____

Individual Profile of Progress: Unit 12

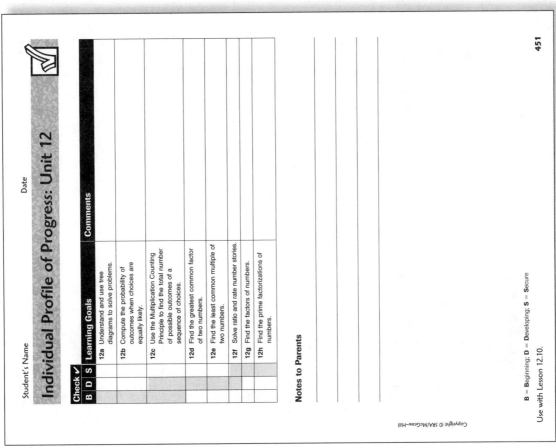

Check ✔			Learning Goals	Comments
B	**D**	**S**		
			12a Understand and use tree diagrams to solve problems.	
			12b Compute the probability of outcomes when choices are equally likely.	
			12c Use the Multiplication Counting Principle to find the total number of possible outcomes of a sequence of choices.	
			12d Find the greatest common factor of two numbers.	
			12e Find the least common multiple of two numbers.	
			12f Solve ratio and rate number stories.	
			12g Find the factors of numbers.	
			12h Find the prime factorizations of numbers.	

Notes to Parents _____

_____

_____

_____

_____

B = **B**eginning; **D** = **D**eveloping; **S** = **S**ecure

Use with Lesson 12.10.

451

Individual Profile of Progress: 1st Quarter

Student's Name _____ Date _____

Check ✔			Learning Goals	Comments
B	**D**	**S**		
			1. Draw arrays to model multiplication. **(1f)**	
			2. Know multiplication facts. **(1g)**	
			3. Identify even and odd numbers. **(1h)**	
			4. Find the factors of numbers. **(1i)**	
			5. Find the sum and difference of multidigit whole numbers and decimals. **(2f)**	
			6. Identify place value in numbers to billions. **(2e, 3f)**	
			7. Use a divisibility test to determine if a number is divisible by another number. **(1c)**	
			8. Identify prime and composite numbers. **(1d)**	
			9. Understand how square numbers and their square roots are related. **(1e)**	
			10. Make magnitude estimates. **(2c)**	
			11. Find the product of multidigit whole numbers and decimals. **(2d)**	
			12. Round numbers to designated places. **(2b)**	
			13. Rename numbers written in exponential notation. **(1b)**	
			14. Find the prime factorizations of numbers. **(1a)**	
			15. Write and solve open sentences for number stories. **(2a)**	
			16. Know properties of polygons. **(3g)**	
			17. Define and create tessellations. **(3h)**	
			18. Estimate the measure of an angle. **(3b)**	
			19. Measure an angle to within 2°. **(3c)**	
			20. Identify types of angles. **(3d)**	

B = Beginning; D = Developing; S = Secure

454

Use with Lesson 3.11.

Class Checklist: 1st Quarter (cont.)

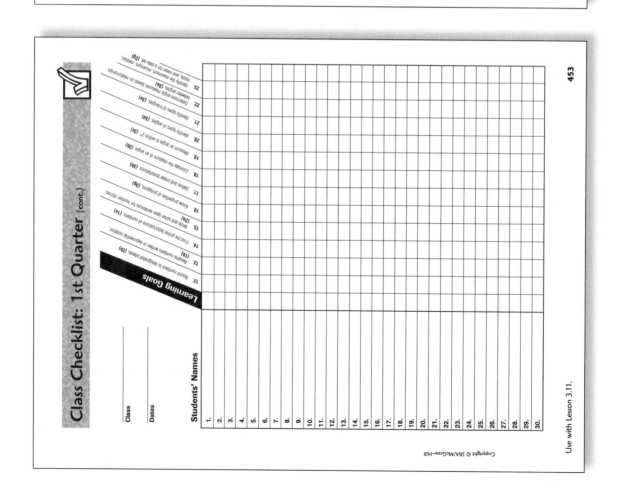

Class _____

Dates _____

Students' Names

Learning Goals:
12. Round numbers to designated places. **(2b)**
13. Rename numbers written in exponential notation. **(1b)**
14. Find the prime factorizations of numbers. **(1a)**
15. Write and solve open sentences for number stories. **(2a)**
16. Know properties of polygons. **(3g)**
17. Define and create tessellations. **(3h)**
18. Estimate the measure of an angle. **(3b)**
19. Measure an angle to within 2°. **(3c)**
20. Identify types of angles. **(3d)**
21. Identify types of triangles. **(3e)**
22. Determine angle measures based on relationships between angles. **(3a)**
23. Identify the maximum, minimum, median, mode, and mean for a data set. **(2g)**

(Students numbered 1. through 30.)

453

Use with Lesson 3.11.

Class Checklist: 2nd Quarter

Class _____

Dates _____

Learning Goals

1. Know place value to hundredths. (4h)
2. Convert between fractions and mixed numbers. (5f)
3. Find equivalent fractions. (5g)
4. Convert between fractions, decimals, and percents. (6g)
5. Find the quotient and remainder a whole number divided by a 1-digit whole number. (4e)
6. Find the quotient and remainder of a whole number divided by a 2-digit whole number. (4e)
7. Make magnitude estimates for quotients of whole and decimal numbers divided by whole numbers. (4d)
8. Interpret the remainder in division number stories. (4f)
9. Determine the value of a variable; use this value to complete a number sentence. (4p)
10. Order and compare fractions. (5a)
11. Convert between fractions and percents. (5c)
12. Add and subtract fractions with like denominators. (5a, 5c)

Students' Names

1.
2.
3.
4.
5.
6.
7.
8.
9.
10.
11.
12.
13.
14.
15.
16.
17.
18.
19.
20.
21.
22.
23.
24.
25.
26.
27.
28.
29.
30.

Use with Lesson 6.11.

456

Student's Name _____   Date _____

Individual Profile of Progress: 1st Quarter

Check ✔			Learning Goals	Comments
B	D	S		
			21. Identify types of angles. (3d)	
			22. Identify types of triangles. (3e)	
			23. Determine angle measures based on relationships between angles. (3a)	
			24. Identify the maximum, minimum, median, mode, and mean for a data set. (2g)	

Notes to Parents

B = Beginning; D = Developing; S = Secure

Use with Lesson 3.11.

455

Individual Profile of Progress: 2nd Quarter

Student's Name _____   Date _____

Check ✓			Learning Goals	Comments
B	**D**	**S**		
			1. Know place value to hundredths. **(4h)**	
			2. Convert between fractions and mixed numbers. **(5f)**	
			3. Find equivalent fractions. **(5g)**	
			4. Convert between fractions, decimals, and percents. **(6g)**	
			5. Find the quotient and remainder of a whole number divided by a 1-digit whole number. **(4c)**	
			6. Find the quotient and remainder of a whole number divided by a 2-digit whole number. **(4d)**	
			7. Make magnitude estimates for quotients of whole and decimal numbers divided by whole numbers. **(4e)**	
			8. Interpret the remainder in division number stories. **(4f)**	
			9. Determine the value of a variable; use this value to complete a number sentence. **(4g)**	
			10. Order and compare fractions. **(5b)**	
			11. Convert between fractions and percents. **(5c)**	
			12. Add and subtract fractions with like denominators. **(5a, 6c)**	
			13. Add and subtract fractions with unlike denominators. **(6d)**	
			14. Find common denominators. **(6f)**	
			15. Divide decimal numbers by whole numbers with no remainders. **(4a)**	
			16. Write and solve number sentences with variables for division number stories. **(4b)**	
			17. Identify and use data landmarks. **(6h)**	
			18. Draw a circle graph for a set of data. **(5d)**	

B = Beginning; **D** = Developing; **S** = Secure

458

Use with Lesson 6.11.

Class Checklist: 2nd Quarter (cont.)

Class _____

Dates _____

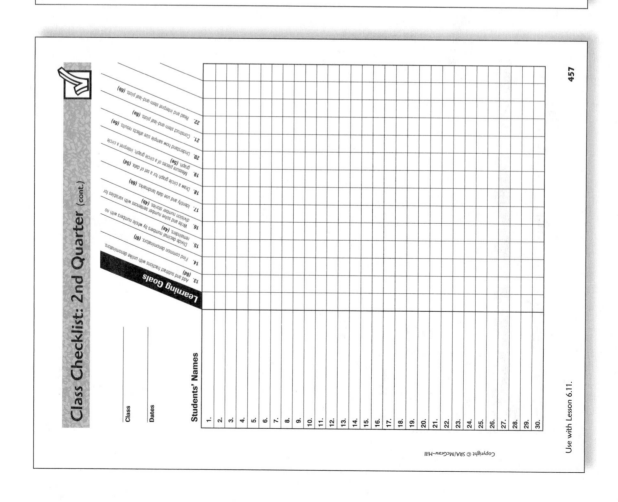

Learning Goals:

13. Add and subtract fractions with unlike denominators. **(6d)**
14. Find common denominators. **(6f)**
15. Divide decimal numbers by whole numbers with no remainders. **(4a)**
16. Write and solve number sentences with variables for division number stories. **(4b)**
17. Identify and use data landmarks. **(6h)**
18. Draw a circle graph for a set of data. **(5d)**
19. Measure pieces of a circle graph; interpret a circle graph. **(5e)**
20. Understand how sample size affects results. **(6e)**
21. Construct stem-and-leaf plots. **(6a)**
22. Read and interpret stem-and-leaf plots. **(6b)**

Students' Names

1.
2.
3.
4.
5.
6.
7.
8.
9.
10.
11.
12.
13.
14.
15.
16.
17.
18.
19.
20.
21.
22.
23.
24.
25.
26.
27.
28.
29.
30.

457

Use with Lesson 6.11.

Class Checklist: 3rd Quarter

Class _____

Dates _____

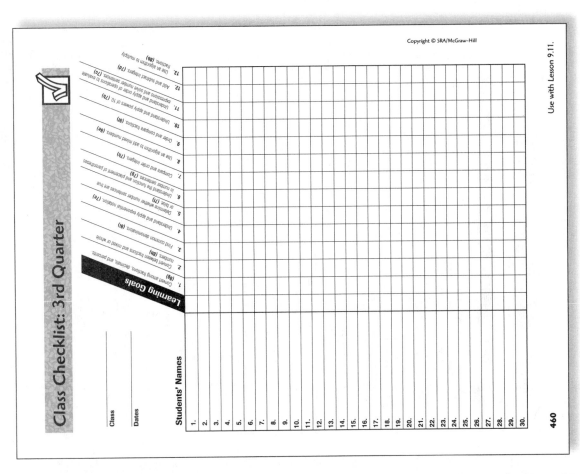

Learning Goals	Students' Names
1. Convert among fractions, decimals, and percents. **(6b)**	
2. Convert between fractions and mixed or whole numbers. **(6b)**	
3. Find common denominators. **(6f)**	
4. Understand and apply exponential notation. **(7e)**	
5. Determine whether number sentences are true or false. **(7f)**	
6. Understand the function and placement of parentheses in number sentences. **(7g)**	
7. Compare and order integers. **(7h)**	
8. Use an algorithm to add mixed numbers. **(6a)**	
9. Order and compare fractions. **(6f)**	
10. Understand and apply powers of 10. **(7b)**	
11. Understand and apply order of operations to evaluate expressions and solve number sentences. **(7c)**	
12. Add and subtract integers. **(7d)**	
13. Use an algorithm to multiply fractions. **(6b)**	

Students' Names: 1. 2. 3. 4. 5. 6. 7. 8. 9. 10. 11. 12. 13. 14. 15. 16. 17. 18. 19. 20. 21. 22. 23. 24. 25. 26. 27. 28. 29. 30.

Use with Lesson 9.11.

460

Copyright © SRA/McGraw–Hill

Student's Name _____   Date _____

Individual Profile of Progress: 2nd Quarter

Check ✔			Learning Goals	Comments
B	D	S		
			19. Measure pieces of a circle graph; interpret a circle graph. **(5e)**	
			20. Understand how sample size affects results. **(6e)**	
			21. Construct stem-and-leaf plots. **(6a)**	
			22. Read and interpret stem-and-leaf plots. **(6b)**	

B = Beginning; **D** = Developing; **S** = Secure

Notes to Parents

Use with Lesson 6.11.

© 2002 Everyday Learning Corporation

459

Individual Profile of Progress: 3rd Quarter

Student's Name ___ Date ___

Check ✔ B	D	S	Learning Goals	Comments
			1. Convert among fractions, decimals, and percents. (8g)	
			2. Convert between fractions and mixed or whole numbers. (8h)	
			3. Find common denominators. (8i)	
			4. Understand and apply exponential notation. (7e)	
			5. Determine whether number sentences are true or false. (7f)	
			6. Understand the function and placement of parentheses in number sentences. (7g)	
			7. Compare and order integers. (7h)	
			8. Use an algorithm to add mixed numbers. (8e)	
			9. Order and compare fractions. (8f)	
			10. Understand and apply powers of 10. (7b)	
			11. Understand and apply order of operations to evaluate expressions and solve number sentences. (7c)	
			12. Add and subtract integers. (7d)	
			13. Use an algorithm to multiply fractions. (8b)	
			14. Use an algorithm to subtract mixed numbers with like denominators. (8c)	
			15. Find a percent of a number. (8d)	
			16. Understand and apply scientific notation. (7a)	
			17. Use an algorithm to multiply mixed numbers. (8a)	
			18. Identify the base and height of triangles and parallelograms. (9e)	
			19. Understand the concept of area of a figure. (9g)	
			20. Use a formula to find the area of rectangles. (9h)	

B = Beginning; D = Developing; S = Secure

462

Use with Lesson 9.11.

Class Checklist: 3rd Quarter (cont.)

Class ___

Dates ___

Learning Goals

14. Use an algorithm to subtract mixed numbers with like denominators. (8c)
15. Find a percent of a number. (8d)
16. Understand and apply scientific notation. (7a)
17. Use an algorithm to multiply mixed numbers. (8a)
18. Identify the base and height of triangles and parallelograms. (9e)
19. Understand the concept of area of a figure. (9g)
20. Use a formula to find the area of rectangles. (8h)
21. Use a formula to find the area of triangles and parallelograms. (9f)
22. Understand the concept of volume of a figure. (9b)
23. Use a formula to find the volume of prisms. (9c)
24. Plot ordered pairs on a one-quadrant coordinate grid. (9d)
25. Plot ordered pairs on a four-quadrant coordinate grid. (9a)

Students' Names
1. 2. 3. 4. 5. 6. 7. 8. 9. 10. 11. 12. 13. 14. 15. 16. 17. 18. 19. 20. 21. 22. 23. 24. 25. 26. 27. 28. 29. 30.

461

Use with Lesson 9.11.

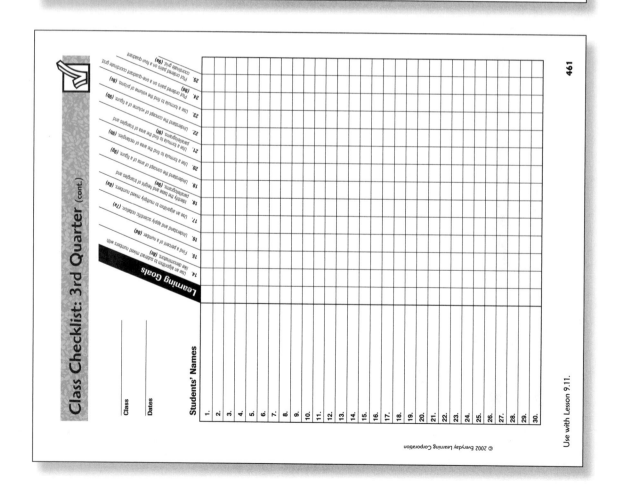

Class Checklist: 4th Quarter

Class _____

Dates _____

Students' Names

Learning Goals

1. Find the factors of numbers. (12a)
2. Find the prime factorizations of numbers. (12b)
3. Solve one-step pan-balance problems. (10l)
4. Solve ratio and rate number stories. (12l)
5. Write algebraic expressions to represent situations. (10b)
6. Represent rate problems as formulas, tables, and graphs. (10e)
7. Find the greatest common factor of two numbers. (12d)
8. Find the least common multiple of two numbers. (12e)
9. Solve two-step pan-balance problems. (10a)
10. Know the properties of geometric solids. (11g)
11. Use formulas to find the area of polygons and circles. (11f)
12. Use formulas to find the volume of prisms and cylinders. (11e)

1. 2. 3. 4. 5. 6. 7. 8. 9. 10. 11. 12. 13. 14. 15. 16. 17. 18. 19. 20. 21. 22. 23. 24. 25. 26. 27. 28. 29. 30.

Use with Lesson 12.10.

464

Student's Name _____   Date _____

Individual Profile of Progress: 3rd Quarter

Check ✓ B D S

Learning Goals	Comments
21. Use a formula to find the area of triangles and parallelograms. (9f)	
22. Understand the concept of volume of a figure. (9b)	
23. Use a formula to find the volume of prisms. (9c)	
24. Plot ordered pairs on a one-quadrant coordinate grid. (9d)	
25. Plot ordered pairs on a four-quadrant coordinate grid. (9a)	

Notes to Parents

B = Beginning; D = Developing; S = Secure

Use with Lesson 9.11.

463

Student's Name _____ Date _____

Individual Profile of Progress: 4th Quarter

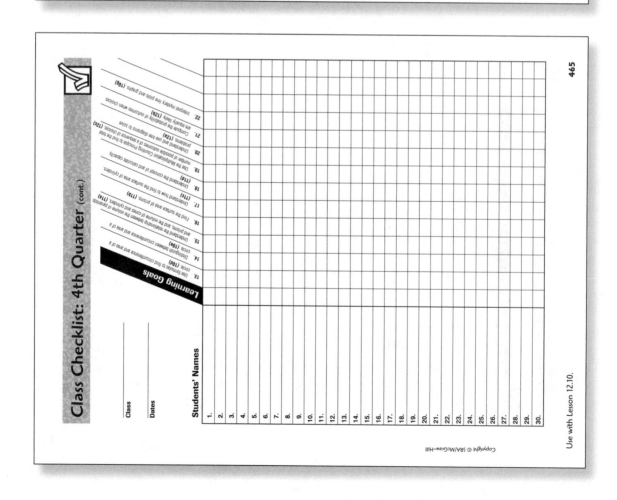

Check ✓			Learning Goals	Comments
B	**D**	**S**		
			1. Find the factors of numbers. (12g)	
			2. Find the prime factorizations of numbers. (12h)	
			3. Solve one-step pan-balance problems. (10f)	
			4. Solve ratio and rate number stories. (12f)	
			5. Write algebraic expressions to represent situations. (10b)	
			6. Represent rate problems as formulas, tables, and graphs. (10c)	
			7. Find the greatest common factor of two numbers. (12d)	
			8. Find the least common multiple of two numbers. (12e)	
			9. Solve two-step pan-balance problems. (10a)	
			10. Know the properties of geometric solids. (11g)	
			11. Use formulas to find the area of polygons and circles. (11f)	
			12. Use formulas to find the volume of prisms and cylinders. (11e)	
			13. Use formulas to find circumference and area of a circle. (10d)	
			14. Distinguish between circumference and area of a circle. (10e)	
			15. Understand the relationship between the volume of pyramids and prisms, and the volume of cones and cylinders. (11a)	
			16. Find the surface area of prisms. (11b)	
			17. Understand how to find the surface area of cylinders. (11c)	
			18. Understand the concept of and calculate capacity. (11d)	
			19. Use the Multiplication Counting Principle to find the total number of possible outcomes of a sequence of choices. (12c)	

B = Beginning; D = Developing; S = Secure

466

Use with Lesson 12.10.

Class Checklist: 4th Quarter (cont.)

Class _____

Dates _____
_____

Learning Goals

12. Use formulas to find circumference and area of a circle. (10d)
13. Distinguish between circumference and area of a circle. (10e)
14. Understand the relationship between the volume of pyramids and prisms, and the volume of cones and cylinders. (11a)
15. Find the surface area of prisms. (11b)
16. Understand how to find the surface area of cylinders. (11c)
17. Understand the concept of and calculate capacity. (11d)
18. Use the Multiplication Counting Principle to find the total number of possible outcomes of a sequence of choices. (12c)
19. Compute the probability of outcomes when choices are equally likely. (12b)
20. Understand and use tree diagrams to solve problems. (12a)
21. Interpret mystery line plots and graphs. (10h)

Students' Names

1.
2.
3.
4.
5.
6.
7.
8.
9.
10.
11.
12.
13.
14.
15.
16.
17.
18.
19.
20.
21.
22.
23.
24.
25.
26.
27.
28.
29.
30.

465

Use with Lesson 12.10.

© 2002 Everyday Learning Corporation

List of Assessment Sources

Ongoing Assessment

Product Assessment

Periodic Assessment

Outside Tests

Other

Use as needed.

468

Student's Name

Date

Individual Profile of Progress: 4th Quarter

Check ✔			Learning Goals	Comments
B	D	S		
			20. Understand and use tree diagrams to solve problems. **(12a)**	
			21. Compute the probability of outcomes when choices are equally likely. **(12b)**	
			22. Interpret mystery line plots and graphs. **(10g)**	

Notes to Parents

B = Beginning; **D** = Developing; **S** = Secure

Use with Lesson 12.10.

Copyright © SRA/McGraw-Hill

467

Class Checklist

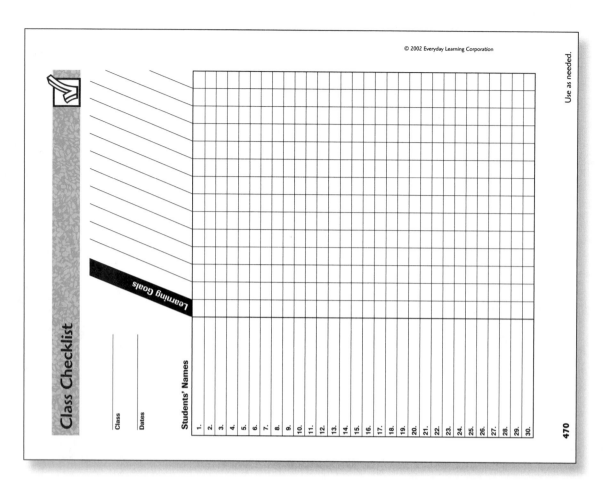

Class _____

Dates _____

Learning Goals

Students' Names

1.
2.
3.
4.
5.
6.
7.
8.
9.
10.
11.
12.
13.
14.
15.
16.
17.
18.
19.
20.
21.
22.
23.
24.
25.
26.
27.
28.
29.
30.

Use as needed.

470

Student's Name _____

Date _____

Individual Profile of Progress

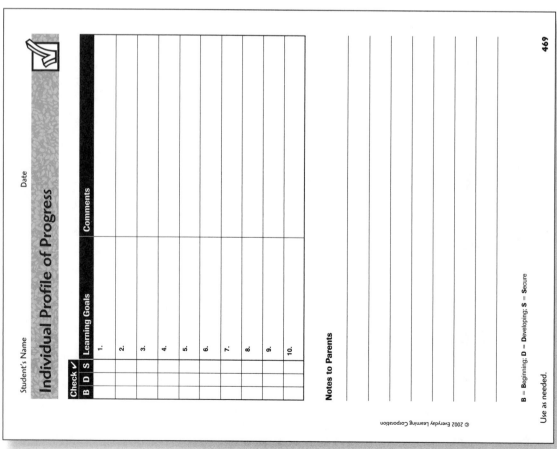

Check ✔			Learning Goals	Comments
B	**D**	**S**		
			1.	
			2.	
			3.	
			4.	
			5.	
			6.	
			7.	
			8.	
			9.	
			10.	

Notes to Parents

B = Beginning; **D** = Developing; **S** = Secure

Use as needed.

469

Evaluating My Math Class

Name _____ Date _____

Interest Inventory

Dislike a Lot	Dislike	Neither Like nor Dislike	Like	Like a Lot
1	2	3	4	5

Use the scale above to describe how you feel about:

1. your math class. _____

2. working with a partner or in a group. _____

3. working by yourself. _____

4. solving problems. _____

5. making up problems for others to solve. _____

6. finding new ways to solve problems. _____

7. challenges in math class. _____

8. playing mathematical games. _____

9. working on Study Links. _____

10. working on projects that take more than a day to complete. _____

11. Which math lesson has been your favorite so far? Why?

_____

_____

_____

_____

_____

Use as needed.

472

Class Progress Indicator

Mathematical Topic Being Assessed: _____

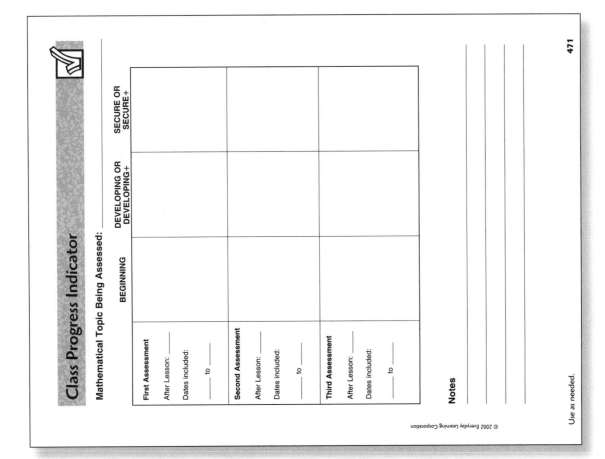

	BEGINNING	DEVELOPING OR DEVELOPING+	SECURE OR SECURE+
First Assessment After Lesson: _____ Dates included: _____ to _____			
Second Assessment After Lesson: _____ Dates included: _____ to _____			
Third Assessment After Lesson: _____ Dates included: _____ to _____			

Notes

_____

_____

_____

_____

Use as needed.

471

Weekly Math Log

Name _____ Date _____

1. What did you study in math this week?

_____

_____

_____

_____

_____

2. Many ideas in math are related to other ideas within math. Think about how the topic(s) you studied in class this week relate to other topics you learned before.

   Your reflection can include what you learned in previous years.

_____

_____

_____

_____

_____

Use as needed.

474

My Math Class

Name _____ Date _____

Interest Inventory

1. In math class, I am good at _____

_____

2. One thing I like about math is _____

_____

3. One thing I find difficult in mathematics class is _____

_____

4. The most interesting thing I have learned in math so far this year is _____

_____

5. Outside school, I used mathematics when I _____

_____

6. I would like to know more about _____

_____

Use as needed.

473

Name _____ Date _____

Number-Story Math Log

1. Write an easy number story that uses mathematical ideas that you have studied recently. Solve the problem.

Number Story

Solution

2. Write a difficult number story that uses mathematical ideas that you have studied recently. If you can, solve the number story. If you are not able to solve it, explain what you need to know to solve it.

Number Story

Solution

Use as needed.

Name _____ Date _____

Math Log

Use as needed.

Name _____ Date _____

Sample Math Work

Self-Assessment

Attach a sample of your work to this form.

1. This work is an example of:

_____
_____
_____
_____
_____

2. This work shows that I can:

_____
_____
_____
_____

OPTIONAL

3. This work shows that I still need to improve:

_____
_____
_____

Use as needed.

477

Name _____ Date _____

Discussion of My Math Work

Self-Assessment

Attach a sample of your work to this page. Tell what you think is important about your sample.

_____
_____
_____
_____
_____
_____
_____
_____
_____
_____
_____
_____

Use as needed.

478

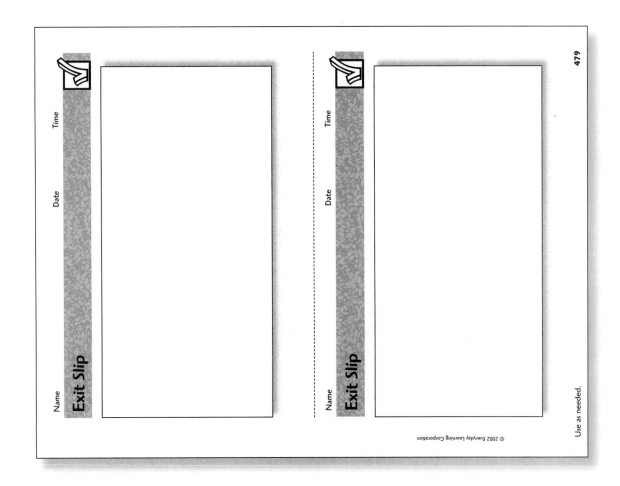

Exit Slip

Name

Date

Time

Exit Slip

Name

Date

Time

© 2002 Everyday Learning Corporation

Use as needed.

479

Glossary

anecdotal records Brief, pertinent pieces of information gathered during informal observation.

assessment The gathering of information about students' progress. This might include their knowledge and use of mathematics, as well as their feelings about their mathematical progress. This information is used to draw conclusions for individual and class instruction.

assessment plan A balanced group of assessment activities chosen by an individual teacher.

assessment sources Mathematical tasks or interactions that can be used for gathering data for assessment purposes.

Class Checklist A tool used to record ongoing observations and interactions.

Class Progress Indicator A form upon which the results of sequential assessment tasks for various mathematical ideas, routines, concepts, and so on, can be recorded for the whole class during the school year using such categories as Beginning, Developing, and Secure.

concepts Basic mathematical ideas that are fundamental in guiding reasoning and problem solving in unfamiliar situations.

evaluation Judgments based on information gathered during assessment.

Individual Profile of Progress A recording tool used to measure the progress of individual students on specific learning goals.

interviews Conversations between a teacher and individual students in which the teacher can obtain information useful for assessing mathematical progress.

long-term projects Mathematical activities that may require time spans of days, weeks, or months to complete.

Math Log A record of a student's mathematical thinking through writing, pictures, diagrams, and so on.

"My Math Class" Inventory A written format for assessing students' attitudes toward mathematics.

observation Watching and recording students' interactions and communications during regular instructional activities.

Ongoing Assessment The gathering of assessment data during regular instructional activities, mostly through observation.

open-ended questions Questions that have multiple answers and strategies for arriving at the answers. (Open-ended questions are good assessments for problem solving and reasoning.)

Outside Tests Usually tests at the school, district, or state level, or nationally standardized tests. If these tests do not match the curriculum, they may not provide valid assessment information.

performance The carrying out or completing of a mathematical activity that displays a student's knowledge and judgment while he or she is engaged in the activity.

Periodic Assessment The more formal gathering of assessment information, often outside of regular instructional time. One example is end-of-unit assessments.

Portfolio A sample collection of a student's mathematical work and related writing representing his or her progress over the school year.

Product Assessment Samples of students' work, which may include pictures, diagrams, or concrete representations.

progress The growth, development, and continuous improvement of students' mathematical abilities.

Progress Indicator See Class Progress Indicator.

reflective writing The ability to reflect and write about mathematics as it relates to accomplishments, confidence, feelings, understanding or lack of understanding, goals, and so on.

representative work A piece of work that represents students' ability and reflects students' progress.

rubric A set of guidelines for scoring assessment activities. The most useful rubrics are those derived from experience with a wide variety of performances on an assessment task.

self-assessment The ability of students to judge, reflect on, acknowledge, and improve the quality of their mathematical thinking or productions.

standardized tests Typically, nationwide tests that are given, scored, and interpreted in a very consistent way, regardless of the population being tested.

strategies The thoughts and procedures an individual student uses to solve a problem.

validity of assessment The degree to which assessment data actually represent the knowledge, thought processes, and skills that students have attained.

Index